THE NEXT STEP

MW01616747

GAIN NEW ENERGY BY LOSING OLD HABITS!

The Next Step to Greater Energy is the book for you if you are ready for new horizons in personal energy. This book presents a new look at habits and addictions, and how they are merely symptoms of a bioenergetic and biochemical imbalance. They call attention to restoring your natural, inherent vitality!

FIND OUT WHAT THESE PEOPLE HAVE IN COMMON

- The perpetual coffee sipper
- The four-soda-a-day drinker
- The tobacco smoker
- The daily marijuana user
- The daily cocktail drinker
- The workaholic
- The compulsive user of salt
- The "speed freak"
- The hard-core heroin addict
- The compulsive jogger
- The secret binge eater
- The constant arguer
- The tobacco dipper
- The loud rock 'n' roller
- The chocolate lover
- The auto-erotic person

All of the above people have a problem, or more positively, an opportunity for self-improvement. Yet they all have different problems—right? Wrong! They are all suffering the consequences of addictive activities: less than optimal health, fatigue, weakened immune systems, depression. All have symptoms of the same dis-ease—an imbalance in the bioenergetic and biochemical systems.

What is an addiction? Is it a disease, an allergy, a weak gene, a self destructive tendency, a way to cope with stress and depression?

Now, in this book, you'll learn what all addictive activities have in common. Only the holistic health approach can encompass all the pieces of the addiction puzzle. *The Next Step to Greater Energy* provides insights into substances and activities that can limit your well-being, AND solutions to breaking free so you, too, can take the next step in your own life-adventure.

THE NEXT STEP TO GREATER ENERGY

A Unique Perspective on Bioenergy, Addictions & Transformation

Jack Tips, ND, PhD

Special thanks for permission to use pictorial information from Health Edco, Waco. Thanks also to Dr. Kenneth Blum, Chief, Division of Alcohol and Substance Abuse, University of Texas Health Science Center, San Antonio and Dr. Michael C. Trachtenberg for permission to quote material from their research on alcohol abuse. Thanks also to Drs. Kenneth Blum, Michael C. Trachtenberg, and Laurel A. Loeblich for permission to quote material from their research on cocaine abuse.

Thanks also to the Los Angeles Times Syndicate for permission to reprint the cartoon from "The Quigmans," and to Chronicle Features for permission to reprint "The Far Side" cartoon by Gary Larson.

Apple-A-Day Press
4201 Bee Caves Road, Suite C212
Austin, Texas 78746-6458
(512) 328-3996

ISBN 0-929167-04-X

Library of Congress Catalog in Publication Card
Number
90-084755

DEDICATION

To the wondrous spirit within
which recognizes no self-limitations
and gives the gentle nudging
to accept greater freedom in our lives.

Jack Tips, ND, PhD

ACKNOWLEDGEMENTS

Many thanks and much gratitude to Dr. Stuart Wheelwright for sharing so much of his life's work with me. The pearls of wisdom he so freely gave have helped me and so many others live a more abundant life.

CONTENTS _____

PREFACE _____

The seed for this book was planted in February, 1986, in Austin, Texas, when I presented a lecture to a gathering of sixty people at the request of a medically oriented health club. The presentation was entitled: "Nutrition to Stop Smoking." The subsequent lengthy question and answer session brought up many important points and stories from the audience concerning health, energy, and addictions.

After the lecture, many people asked for copies of the taped presentation. As is often the case when someone uses a portable cassette recorder to tape a presentation, the tape quality was quite poor. Therefore we provided a transcript of the lecture minus the "ums" and "ers."

Since many vital messages about fatigue, energy, self-improvement, and addiction were also contained in the question and answer session—which was not taped—I decided to write additional information to accompany the transcription and to add some background. Insight Press printed the information in a booklet, entitled *Energy & Addictions* (1986).

After *Energy & Addictions* was printed, two things happened that led to its second edition. In 1987, on four occasions, different people approached me in the crowded aisles of Whole Foods Market, on the Zilker Park hike-and-bike trail, here at the Systemic Clinic, or at Mother's Cafe and Garden, a natural foods restaurant in Austin. They said: "I just wanted you to know that I read your book and broke my cocaine addiction;" and "I was able to quit smoking by following your book;" and "We got sugar out of the house, now our allergies cleared up and Tommy isn't hyperkinetic anymore;" and "I gave your book to my husband; he's quit drinking." Of course, it was rewarding for me to know that a new idea can help someone, and that writing about it contributed to such changes.

Since the second edition sold out quickly, and because additional insights into bioenergy and its connection to energy impostors and addictions have become more clearly defined, the current third edition was produced. This third edition has been expanded to contain much new information including comments from clients, insights from other researchers, and even material which was thought too controversial for the initial draft.

The book's title was changed to *The Next Step to Greater Energy* to express the value of the information for anyone desiring to break out of old life-patterns and grow into a greater awareness of what he or she can be. Such awareness inescapably leads to greater, natural energy.

The focus of this book is a compassionate examination of addictive behaviors and not simply a discourse on the evils of such activities. This book was always intended to be an informative look at the many substances and activities which commonly inhibit our personal energy and often our spiritual growth, and to recognize them as teachers from which to learn. The very things which tend to shackle our wondrous spirit are the lessons we need to learn—lessons such as independence, self-reliance, attainment of goals, rejection of illusions, and embracement of reality. These lessons are the testing ground by which we prove our worthiness to accept more freedom and responsibility in our lives.

This book is written for individuals who wish to gain an overview of the Natural Laws of Life as they relate to the human spirit's quest for freedom, health, and abundance. The forum by which we organize this discussion is the topic of addictions and addictive activities, since participation in addictive practices often limits a person's ability to experience the full and varied dimensions of a truly fulfilling life.

It is my expectation that *The Next Step to Greater Energy* serve as a springboard for those individuals who are ready to take the next step in an endless progression of steps toward self-mastery.

Austin, Texas, July, 1990
Jack Tips

1

BIOENERGY: A NEW PERSPECTIVE ON UNDERSTANDING AND ENDING ADDICTIONS

AN UNDERSTANDING OF BIOENERGY

By presenting the concept of BIOENERGY and its relationship to biochemistry, this book offers a new perspective on the phenomena of addictions and addictive activities. From this unique perspective on the bioenergetic connection to addictions comes new knowledge and understanding for achieving freedom from addictions and living a more fulfilled life.

This book offers perspectives that are distinctly different from other addiction treatment and relief programs, because this material is based on clinically applied therapies, designed for the complete and uniquely individual person. Another reason for the distinctive difference is that such programs incorporate the adjustment of the disturbed bioenergetic forms, as presented in addictive lifestyles, in addition to basic biochemical support with specific nutrients.

The knowledge about bioenergetics is an effective tool as well as a powerful ally in overcoming the helpless, codependent, futile, self-destructive relationships with pain-alleviating addictive behaviors. This knowledge also is important to defeat the entrapping, artificial, elective poisons which encompass the energy-igniting addictions. All addictive behaviors, whether for pain relief or extra energy, inhibit the full, creative expression of the individual and thus are expressions of limitations, of something alien, to the innate bioenergetic blueprint.

It does not matter whether the issues underlying addictive behaviors are physical, emotional, mental, or spiritual issues. They all can be solved by understanding and applying the concepts of bioenergy, because the one common denominator of all illness, all disease, all lack or want, all degenerations, and all unhappiness is a disruption of the bioenergetic flow cellularly, individually, globally.

A BRIEF PHILOSOPHICAL HISTORY OF BIOENERGY FROM EASTERN AND WESTERN TRADITIONS

The new perspective, or overview, introduced here is called BIOENERGY. This term means LIFE FORCE and refers to the bioelectric field of the human body which is comprised of two dynamic and interactive parts: the positive and the negative fields. For thousands of years, the Chinese have referred to these two aspects of the bioelectric field as "yang" and "yin." Currently, even modern Western medical experts recognize the important medical significance of these vibrational, electric fields for the human body, as discussed, for example, by Dr. Richard Gerber (M.D.) in his perceptive book, *Vibrational Medicine* (1988). Robert O. Becker (M.D.) claims as well that the new paradigm of life energy may well be the "hidden dynamic in medicine," as he portrays the role of bioenergetics in healing the body.

The basic premise underlying the concept of bioenergy means that an individual is actually a manifestation of the universal life force. The physical aspect of this life force is called "ch'i" or "ki" in ancient Eastern terms. This life force is, in essence, a person's life or spirit.

The notion of bioenergy is not at all novel in Western philosophical tradition. The Greek philosopher Aristotle (340 B.C.) recognized the life force principle as the moving universal power. Centuries later, the French philosopher Henry Bergson (1859-1941) coined the term "Elan Vital", signifying the life energy. His notion became widely accepted in the Western world. Bergson, just like Aristotle, also considered the elan vital to be the universal vital force giving shape and energy to all life forms, including the human body.

Although philosophically the concept of bioenergy has been part of the Western tradition, medically it was generally ignored and not implemented or accepted until recently due to its lack of a biochemical basis. At this juncture of human knowledge, the Eastern traditions have much to offer the West for treatment of disease from the bioenergetic perspective. In turn, the West has much to offer the East from a biochemical basis.

Total health means that the life force is free-flowing and synergistically supportive of its dual aspects, the positive and negative bioelectric fields. Any blockage or excess in the inherent character of the bioenergetic field causes dis-ease or discomfort.

With this brief introduction, we can now make a model of a human being. First, there exists the all pervasive life force, also called the vital spirit, which animates all life. The dynamic characteristic of the life force is that it flows out from, and back to, its universal source, and only in its presence is there life. When the life force flow becomes organized into specific oscillations, the bioenergetic matrix of a person is formed.

How such organization of the life force actually occurs has been the topic of lengthy scientific debates. The most current view, which has caused much discussion, was formulated by the eminent British biochemist Rupert Sheldrake in his book, *The Presence of the Past. Morphic Resonance and the Habits of Nature* (1988). In his first book, *A New Science of Life* (1981), Sheldrake decisively questioned the traditional Western view of a mechanical origin of the cosmos, nature, and man. Instead, Sheldrake speculates that morphic resonance fields guide the development of forms

Since the topic of the organization of life force is too extensive and complex for our discussion at hand, we will proceed with considering the manifestation of the life force as found in and around the human body. This is the bioenergetic principle we will examine in this book.

The bioenergetic matrix of the life force represents the human body. Consequently, the body has a bioenergetic flow within it, a positive and a negative flow. The positive energy flows out, and the negative energy flows back in; and the energy circulates in the body as long as the covenant of life is

operative. Within this dynamic energy field we each constitute our being for the duration of the field's organization, and
operate our bodies within it.

We have spoken of these fundamental bioenergetic principles in the dispassionate terms of science and avoided the
spiritual implications. Aristotle called the life force the "soul."
But if we were to refer to the life force as "God," or the "Holy
Spirit," many scientists would dismiss this discussion immediately. Whatever the life force is called, it continues its effects, and its principles that we are discussing hold true.

The bioenergetic concept at the physical level is very
similar to a magnet which has both a positive and negative
pole. We could also make an analogy to the earth which has
a south and north pole. The body is a microcosm of the earth,
and the earth is a microcosm of the universe. This concept
continues on into infinity. Within the body, the cells are a microcosm of the body. Consequently, the variations of this
representational theme go both ways.

Within this bioenergetic flow resides the human form of
flesh and bones, brain and feelings, lymph and blood. And
within the bioenergetic matrix, or form of flesh and bones, are
the biochemical systems that we are more familiar with. These
biochemical systems are digestion, Kreb's cycle energy, pH
balance, immune responses, and myriad enzyme reactions and
hormonal processes which operate and regulate the physical
body.

Our working definition of bioenergy places it into the dimension of the scientifically documented electrical field of the
body. And, for background information we included the perspective of Eastern philosophy. Rather than simply define the
body as the traditional test tube of chemical reactions, the
bioenergy concept actually describes and accounts for the
etheric forces which comprise every life form and have a fundamental role in life, health, and health maintenance.

This overview of the body as a bioenergetic force in
contrast to viewing the body as a mechanical system, is like
viewing a fish in context of the ocean which supports it, and
not just as a function of its gills and fins.

BIOENERGY PLUS BIOCHEMISTRY EQUAL THE WHOLE PERSON

Ultimately, there are two basic and fundamental body systems involved with addictions and addictive activities: the bioenergetic and the biochemical. Most people are generally familiar with their body's biochemical system and its biochemical reactions. If people eat salt, they get thirsty; if they take aspirin, the headache is relieved; if they drink a gallon of carrot juice a day, their skin turns orange; if they drink too much whisky, they pass out; if they eat a meal, hunger vanishes. All of these occurrences are basically biochemical reactions.

Sciences which specialize in human biochemistry include biochemistry, biology, medicine, orthomolecular nutrition (vitamins, minerals, enzymes, amino acids, lipids), and modem herbology (phyto-pharmacologics). These sciences have given us great insights into addictions by isolating various chemicals which cause reactions in the body, and by observing and documenting the effects of chemicals on various tissues as well.

Our current information on the physiological aspects of the addictive phenomenon comes from the findings of these sciences. This is the Western philosophy of hard, scientific facts regarding the processes of the physical body. These are facts which can be duplicated the world over. And we will discuss many findings from the perspective of biochemistry since it represents the most readily available reality of what is occurring in our bodies.

But we have now learned that this physical body of biochemical processes exists in an ocean of energy, and that this bioenergetic ocean has laws and characteristics which govern and effect the biochemical process. Consequently, we are advancing a major step in our understanding of the forces at work in our lives.

Sciences which specialize in treating the human bioenergy field include homeopathy, systemic herbology, acupuncture, electro-acupuncture, and their offshoots. These sciences are advancing the validity of energy as medicine.

5

As more knowledge and understanding of the bioenergetic workings of the living body are discovered, we must continue to redefine the concept of health. We soon learn that health is a dynamic state, not a static goal to be held on to. Health is simply the balance of the free-flowing bioenergetic field. This balance results in, and is dependent on, the balance of the biochemical processes of the body.

An important definition of health is provided by Paul Twitchell. In his book, *Herbs the Magic Healers* (1988), Twitchell discusses what is required to return health to the body: "Health comes, of course, with the adjustment of the vibratory rates within one's self". He defines health as follows: "Health and happiness means to be rid of fatigue and disease. To have a good appetite, good memory, good humor, and precision in thought and action. To be free from anxiety and fear. To have a great capacity for survival over illness and anxieties. To have joy, long life, and great spiritual adventures."

What we are discussing is the synergistic relationship between the bioenergetic and biochemical aspects of a human being. This is not quite a "chicken or the egg" situation, since the energy, or the life force, had to exist first, but both systems affect each other. This means that health is a balance of both systems. This also means that to be truly effective in the cure of disease, a health practitioner must be able to work with both systems and help the patient restore whole balance.

Not many people in the Western hemisphere are familiar with the bioenergetic sciences primarily because bioenergy is invisible and cannot be contained in a test tube, which continues as the standard for Western scientific reality. The illusive bioenergetic pathways of the body are just now being recognized by Western science for two reasons: 1) the development and healing applications of sensitive, electronic equipment (thanks to Dr. Reinhold Voll, the father of electro-acupuncture) which can measure, chart, and affect the bioenergetic flow through a person's body; and 2) scientists can no longer deny the obvious evidence and results of bioenergetic support to the body.

Basically, Western science is just now catching up to what the Chinese have been documenting for 5000 years in their medical system. And in the process of catching up to other medical paradigms, Western science has made quantum leaps into understanding the biochemistry of the body. Although admittedly, Western scientists are slow to recognize, or accept, the important bioenergetic features of such new paradigms.

Meanwhile, in the United States, the special interests of the large drug companies, and the professional unions that govern many practitioners, have directly inhibited and persecuted expansion into this area of healing, because bioenergetic medicines are competitive, and usually more effective, alternatives. By now the public outcries about the increasingly ineffective medical system in the United States are public record.

Yet, in Great Britain, the Royal Family continues using homeopathic medicine, one of the primary bioenergetic medicines. And, in Germany, a renewed interest in its native homeopathic and herbal health systems is currently leading to an increase in course offerings in homeopathy and herbology for medical training at the medical schools.

Homeopathy is the premier bioenergetic science as it can work in deeper to a persons bioenergy than any science known to man at this time. For those yet unfamiliar with homeopathy as an alternative to dangerous, chemical drugs, a brief definition is provided here. Homeopathy is a method of using microdoses of natural substances to treat illness. The word "homeopathy" means "like suffering." Its principle assigns therapeutic remedies to patients based on matching the symptom picture with the remedy which would produce the same symptoms if taken in gross amounts.

Homeopathic medicines, as a rule, are non-toxic and produce no poisonous side effect as is so often the case with drug therapies. This fact has earned homeopathic remedies the reputation of being safe, natural, and effective. Homeopathy has effected millions of cures for humanity's myriad diseases such as asthma, epilepsy, skin disorders, allergic states, mental and emotional disorders, and hormonal imbalances.

In his fascinating discussion of homeopathic remedies as vibrational medicines, Gerber suggests that during the homeopathic preparation of plants their physical drug properties are removed. But the plants' subtle-energy qualities are absorbed by the water or alcohol medium to predominate. Gerber further suggests that Hahnemann produced an energetic frequency match between the homeopathic remedy and the patient. According to Gerber, certain studies indicate that changes in a person's etheric energy body precede disease in the patient's physical body. Therefore we can assume that healing also needs to effect the subtle energy level before disease patterns are changed. To effect such changes appears to be the major advantage of homeopathic remedies.

Homeopathy was founded by Dr. Samuel Hahnemann in Germany in the early 1800's. Its popularity has waxed and waned throughout the world since its inception. Homeopathy has been actively persecuted in the United States by the American Medical Association. Currently there are more than 6000 medical doctors practicing homeopathy in France, and thousands of others practice it throughout Europe and the rest of the world. At this point in time, homeopathy is experiencing a tremendous, long overdue resurgence in the United States.

The bioenergetic science which works specifically to manipulate the body's bioelectrical field is acupuncture which practices the insertion of thin needles into the body. This is the ancient system of healing and health maintenance, based on the balance of the body's bioenergetic meridian pathways. Imbalances in the meridian flow of energy affect the corresponding organs. Reciprocally, stresses in the affected organs, glands, and tissues affect the bioenergetic balance.

Acupuncture and its related, non-invasive sciences such as reflexology, shiatsu, Touch for Health, electro-acupuncture, and certain aspects of chiropractic, work to restore balance to the body via the meridian system and nerve flow. It is noteworthy that some major medical insurance companies have recently begun to pay for acupuncture and chiropractic treatment, signaling an important recognition of the value of such bioenergetic treatments.

The premier nutritional bioenergetic science is systemic herbology founded by A.S. Wheelwright (1918-1990). Wheelwright cataloged the bioenergetic resonance patterns of the various body tissues, glands, and organs, and constructed synergistic herbal combinations to approximate those precise patterns. To construct such formulas, Wheelwright combined herbs, vitamins, minerals, enzymes, amino acids, protomorphagins, and other nutrient factors into bioenergetically and biochemically balanced nutrients. By doing so, he pioneered the concept of "balanced therapy" which means that the formulas are balanced in themselves and work to restore balance in the targeted tissue, its related system, and ultimately the whole body. Thus, people with a hypo or hyper condition can be helped by the identical formula, because a bioenergetically balanced formula assists the body to normalize any imbalance whether it be under- or over-active.

To repeat, we need to understand that a bioenergetic imbalance affects the body's biochemistry, and that an imbalance in the body's biochemistry in turn affects the body's bioenergy system. With a better understanding of these processes we are obtaining a more "whole-istic", or by common usage "holistic", view of our bodies.

Unfortunately, the word "holistic" is bandied about much like the word "natural" these days. Therefore, its meaning is largely becoming undefinable and abused. For this reason we establish our own definition: holistic pertains to, and is compatible with, the whole person and all synergistic parts, including the physical dimension (bioenergetic and bio-chemical); the emotional dimension; the causative forces (imagination); the mental and innate tacit agreements with reality; and the spiritual dimensions.

The synthesis of Eastern knowledge and Western science is opening new doors to healing and maintaining a healthy body. It remains unfortunate that many Western scientists and physicians continue to be slow in recognizing such important knowledge. In the interest of your own as health, it is highly recommended to become familiar with alternative practices and to support the legitimate organizations dedicated to protecting your freedom to choose the health care you desire.

EXAMPLES OF THE BIOENERGETIC EFFECT

Although people from Western cultures are generally unfamiliar with the body's bioenergetic system, many have experienced instances of its presence. A common experience is noticing a pain in a reflex zone in the feet. For example, right before a recurring bladder infection, some people notice a tenderness in the arch of the foot, in the bladder zone. Or a person may feel "at odds" when sleeping in the room next to an electrical transformer, because an unnatural force field emanates from transformers and disrupts the body's sensitive bioenergetic field.

Another common example of experiencing a bioenergetic field occurs, when a person is exposed to television screen emanations while working at computer terminals, or watching color TV. In fact, most of the stress, associated with operating computers, is the disruption of the operator's bioenergetic field by the stream of radiation coming out of the monitor which is a cathode ray tube or television set. Excessive exposure to pregnant women is linked with miscarriages. Such research has been reported by Becker (1990).

People have noticed instant relief from such bioenergetic stress by adding a diode to their screen which absorbs the radiation and ends their eye fatigue, malaise, and out of sorts feelings. Some people use lead glass shields which can be purchased at computer supply stores.

Fluorescent light tubes also cause bioenergetic problems which compound the problem of T.V. radiation, because the light tubes emit a strong, bioenergetically disruptive force field at both ends of the tube. Such lights give off only partial spectrum light, because the fluorescent light spectrum leans to either the pink or blue ends of the color spectrum. There are now companies which make full-spectrum light bulbs that are well documented to help with the problem of working indoors in artificial light. An insightful discussion about the effects of light on human health is provided by John Ott in the book, *Light, Radiation and You* (1985).

The extent to which such fluorescent lighting can affect the body's bioenergetic field is depicted by the following anecdotal case history from clinical practice. A 20-year old female bank receptionist suddenly developed acne as diagnosed by her family physician. Since the onset was sudden, it would not be in error to assume that "something" caused the condition, and that a quick correction would remedy it in a short time. The client preferred to try natural remedies first rather than take the drug Acutane, because malaise and fatigue accompanied her work day, although she was fine on the weekends, suggesting a stressful period of adjustment to her new job. Her SMAC-25, CBC, blood test showed to be normal with no out-of-range values. Liver enzymes were low normal.

The standard nutritional considerations were implemented with complete compliance: no fried foods, no sugar, no caffeine, no alcohol. And the Pro-Vita! Plan—as described in the book, *The Pro-Vita! Diet* (Tips, 1989)—with digestive supplements was followed to guarantee proper digestion of proteins in case the acne was a protein allergy. Broad-base nutritional supplementation with natural vitamins and minerals in an herbal base was also supplied.

The therapy centered around blood cleansing endeavors via The Liver Triad (digestion, elimination, and liver support)—discussed in the book, *The Liver Triad* (Tips, 1989)—and hormonal stabilization via systemic herbology for the female endocrine system. The homeopathic remedy Sepia 9c was given because the client portrayed its characteristic symptom-picture in the acute.

There was an immediate positive response to the program as expected, and another grateful client—until the 30-day program expired. Then the acne came back, ruining the client's new-employee-recognition ceremony.

The program was begun again, modified to focus on more specific areas suspected of being the cause. The female endocrine support was omitted, because the client had no further corroborating symptoms, such as PMS, or dysmennorhea. Since beginning the program, noticeable improvement in previous menstrual problems occurred.

Again, as before, there was immediate response to the nutritional therapy, and happiness restored—until the client quit the reduced supplement program. And after six weeks of perfect complexion, suddenly the acne reappeared.

At this point we acknowledged several things: 1) something was causing the acne; 2) nutrition was working, but not curing; 3) the client was fully compliant with the Pro-Vita! Diet; 4) her blood chemistry was normal; 5) as a working mother she could not afford to spend a lot of money each month on supplements or continued counsel; and 6) that nutritional work had an element of trial and error.

Then, one afternoon I went to open an account at the bank where the client worked. She greeted me with a smile through heavy makeup and turned me over to the new accounts department. After a few minutes in the bank and noticing its layout and lighting, I went over to the client, and explained that I thought I had the answer to her acne problem and to drop by the clinic for one supplement.

She received a Vitamin A complex in an herbal formula designed for the eyes. Her complexion cleared up again, though it lingered on the verge of breaking out, in her opinion. She continued on this formula for two months, until she was ready to consult again.

Of course, her question was: "What's going on?" coupled with the concern: "Do I have to keep taking supplements to avoid acne?"

I explained to her the cause for her acne. The cause was found in the environment of her work. The bank where she worked was located in the middle of a sky scraper office building. The bank had no windows and featured only fluorescent light. What was occurring with her was that the artificial, pink-spectrum light in the work space was disrupting the bioenergetic rhythms of her body, causing bioenergetic stress. As well, this light was robbing her body of excessive amounts of Vitamin A, used by her eyes. This same situation occurs also with water and snow skiers when they are exposed to the bright reflected light during their sport. The exposure to such bright light represents a biochemical stress.

Over the course of the next six months, the client took a vacation from work and from the supplemental eye formula. She experienced no acne. Upon returning to work, however, the acne reappeared, until she took the natural Vitamin A (Eye) supplement.

To my client's good fortune, the bank was bought out, and she was transferred to a wonderful, open, light-filled environment. In this new work space she had no further problems with acne.

This client's case is an example where an energetic factor was a contributing cause to the health problem. The fluorescent lights' detrimental energy disrupted her bioenergetic system, as evidenced by her malaise and fatigue. In addition, these lights caused a biochemical deficit of Vitamin A which resulted in the disturbing symptom of acne—the body's cry for balance.

Other common items which are disruptive of the body's bioenergetic force field include electric clocks, electric razors, hair dryers, microwave ovens, electric heaters, water bed heaters, electric blankets, and so forth. Appliances which are plugged into the wall and operate on an electric motor generate electric fields which can interfere with human health. Appliances which operate on batteries create much smaller fields and are much less disturbing. For this reason electro-acupuncture diagnostic equipment must operate on a battery and is not plugged into a wall socket.

Now we continue with our discourse on bioenergy and addictions. Those of you with further interest in the effects of light and electrical emanations on human health, can follow up with your own studies on this fascinating and extensive subject.

BIOENERGY: THE COMMON THREAD IN ADDICTIONS

Addictions constitute a serious health and social problem in our society. In this book we share with you the principles and therapies that we use to help people break the ties with their self-limiting, addictive behaviors.

To give you a preview, true healing therapies provide bioenergetic support by adjusting the wave form that manifests as the human form, as well as provide a solid foundation in the health triad of attitude, structure, and nutrition. When a therapy program addresses the whole addiction pattern, success is assured. This book will inform you about never-before-published insights into addictions and show you how to let them drop away naturally, effectively, permanently, profoundly! It will also show you how to replace the addictions with natural vitality, joy, enthusiasm, and new purpose in life.

The most important aspect of this book concerns bioenergy. Therefore, this book is really about bioenergy, the least familiar concept for most people, and bioenergy's connection with addictive behaviors and substances. During recent years, with an increasing social drug problem, many different programs have offered help to overcome addictive behaviors, but their success rates have not been high. Only those programs which base their treatment on the common thread that runs through all addictive behaviors offer lasting help.

The common thread in all addictions involves bioenergy, the subtle energy wave forms that are as much a part of the human being as the brains and the kidneys. In effect, all diseases are first a disruption of the body's bioenergetic pattern. This disruption can be caused by attitude, thoughts and feelings, as well as biochemistry, that is, the lack or excess of nutrients, or chemicals introduced into the body.

Bioenergy is now widely recognized by the healing professions, and is actually the way of the future for the health sciences, also. Richard Gerber, for example, in his book, *Vibrational Medicine* (1988), views energy medicine and Einsteinian physics in opposition to traditional medicine and Newton's mechanical physics. Clearly, bioenergy is the next vital step in planetary and personal healing, because its great potentials come at a time when we stand virtually on the threshold of peril in a world filled with nuclear and various microwave radiations, toxic wastes, poisoned air, depleted soil, toxic drugs, barbaric surgeries, depleted ozone, and contaminated water. Mankind is about to understand the natural laws of life and to undo the effects of ignorance that have lead us to the current precarious environmental situation.

Since bioenergy is the common thread running through all addictive behaviors, only those healing therapies which address this commonality offer viable pathways for all dependent people and provide profound results. Without an understanding of the common thread, therapies to help break addictions fall short of initiating true healing responses. This fact is evidenced by the pattern that many people follow of merely substituting other activities for their initial addiction. For example, people will stop using alcohol, but increase smoking and sugar intake; or become hooked on group meetings and group therapies; or return to addictive behaviors and patterns once again. These substitutions of other activities for the initial addictive activity happen, because the underlying bioenergetic and biochemical imbalances were not corrected.

The programs discussed in this book feature as a key success factor the reestablishing of a person's bioenergy to take over for the pseudo energy created by the addictive substances. How addictions create such pseudo energy is discussed in a later chapter. But the entire discussion is really about bioenergy and how to reestablish it in the addictive person, even though we will often discuss at length the biochemical processes associated with addictions as well.

To restate, the bioenergetic blueprint for the human being is a free-flowing, perpetual wave form connected to the universal subtle energies. An aberration disturbs the oscillations and thus creates a less than optimal pattern. Such a disturbance is the highest common denominator, or common thread, of all addictive behaviors. The level at which the aberration occurs determines the characteristic and individual manifestation of the less-than-optimal pattern, or in this case, an addictive tendency.

With some people the disturbance is an hereditary shortage of endorphins in the brain. With others it is an imbalance in the physical energy system. With some persons the disturbance is a nutritional/biochemical imbalance; in others it is an acquired habit or affliction. With still other people the disturbance represents an apparent way to cope with the stress of living, or an attempt to establish a normal pattern in an abnormal life-style.

Aberrations, or disturbances, in the bioenergetic field that surrounds all life forms are known to be the beginnings of practically every disease. Addictive behaviors, whether they are exemplified by a need to use heroin or a craving for sugar, are both symptoms and causes of bioenergetic aberrations. And, they contribute to further aberrations that ultimately become diseases.

Whether we attribute addictions to heredity, environment, karma, luck of the draw, a disease, an allergy, a proclivity, a compulsion, a tendency, a weakness—it does not matter. When addictions are addressed comprehensively and the therapies are verified bioenergetically, then people can effect both cure and repair in their lives.

True healing therapies provide, in addition to the bioenergetic support, a solid foundation in the health triad of attitude, structure, and nutrition. Such programs also help the client with "roll-up-your-sleeves" type of constructive efforts to overcome addictions.

In clinical practice we work with people's addictive behaviors daily as do alternative practitioners worldwide. Our success rate is certainly as high as in the facilities that are solely dedicated to breaking addictions. One reason for our success is the commitment of people who seek nutritional, alternative, and holistic counsel. Their first step is of their own effort and initiative.

Moreover, these persons often must receive such therapies at their own expense, since the major insurance companies blatantly exclude the natural therapies from reimbursement of costs. In this way insurance companies deny people financial assistance to work alternatively and further lock them into the morass of drugs and invasive medicine. The clients' desire and commitment to work alternatively contributes greatly to their success in our program. The rest is up to the program to balance their bioenergetic disturbances and normalize the biochemical processes.

Of course, there are many interlocking, shifting pieces to the addiction puzzle—a puzzle that represents challenges to our health, life expectancy, and the quality of our life experience. There is sound evidence that clearly describes the biochemical, allergic, psychological, emotional (for example, depression), hereditary, bioenergetic, stress-induced, and nutritional pieces of the puzzle. But what pieces apply to which person at what time? Finding the answer to this important question is the artistry of the natural health therapies! We will discuss this topic throughout the book.

2

HEALING THE WHOLE PERSON

THE REAL ISSUE

Most people caught up in addiction cycles do not really get free. They substitute one addiction for another. The alcoholic may substitute cigarettes and coffee for alcohol. The smoker may substitute coffee and carbohydrate or sugar foods. The sugar addict may cut back on sugar but increase coffee. The coffee addict may exchange a coffee addiction for sweets and compulsive jogging.

It is true, of course, that the addiction substitute may be better or more healthy than the addiction itself and a step in the right direction. An alcoholic who switches to cigarettes, coffee, and sugar has made a tremendous improvement. Alcoholism is terribly damaging. And breaking such an addiction is a vitally important step because it can reopen lines of communication with family members, encourage greater self-esteem, and offers the promise of a brighter, healthier future.

This book is for people who want to go all the way, who want to live their lives ONE HUNDRED PERCENT and be free of all addictions and their limitations. All addictive behaviors, no matter how diverse or socially acceptable, have a great deal in common. By understanding this, a way to be free from all addictive patterns becomes evident, possible, and practical. This means to be able to experience life many steps removed from these severely limiting patterns.

In the Preface we learned that the seed concept for this material came from a discussion during a lecture on nutrition to stop smoking.

During the question and answer session, many questions and comments such as the following came up. "Well, what's so wrong with addictions? God gave us a body with that capability built in!" "Aren't we all addicted to air and food?" "I'm addicted to women who mother me." "The more weight I gained the more unloved I felt, and eating chocolate helped me cope with that feeling, but kept making me fatter."

One woman had introduced herself by saying: "I'm Martha, I quit drinking three years ago. I'm an alcoholic." That comment really caught me!

"No, you are not an alcoholic!" I replied a little harshly, surprising even myself. "You are a soul who's escaped a self-destructive, self-limiting pattern. Quit identifying with your diseases and identify with your goals for a new, vibrant, successful, meaningful life."

"Unlike a paraplegic who cannot lead a normal life, you CAN lead a normal life. Alcohol consumption is not a normal aspect of life. You're just more susceptible than others, but great repair can be effected nutritionally."

Then, to temper my comment I added: "Being honest and bringing your condition out of the closet is a big step. Your victory over alcohol was and is a valuable experience. Now, why not build even more with that pattern for success which you've established by winning your freedom from alcohol. You succeeded at stopping. Success breeds success, you know. So look ahead to what you will be, not behind at what you were."

"The more a person affirms things like, 'I am a diabetic, I am an asthmatic, I am an alcoholic; the more they hold on to that reality. Personally speaking, I am a person who'll die from a lack of oxygen, but I don't go around affirming that every day. You may be terribly susceptible to alcohol. Your endorphins may all be blown away by even one drop of alcohol whereas other people can repair the damage of alcohol in their brains. But that sensitivity can be helped a great deal with nutrition. And every year it gets better! You may never get over your extreme sensitivity to alcohol, and I may never get over dying without oxygen, but both us can live abundant lives despite the limitations of our physical bodies."

Martha replied: "I see what you're saying. The reason I'm here tonight is to look ahead, as you put it, and I just want to say that what's helped me the most tonight was to hear your idea that the body uses addictions to get the energy it needs. I wanted to add that love is an energy, too—and I can feel the love in what you just said to me—and if people can forgive others and love themselves and God, then all things are possible. It's even possible for me to quit smoking now that I've broken my dependence on alcohol!"

What we were finally discussing was much more than nutrition. We were dealing with the most basic tenet of holistic health care: we were talking about healing the whole person, not just restricting habits.

Two years after the lecture, I read the booklet *Energy & Addictions* again wondering, "What is it about these facts and theories that are helping people get in touch with their own healing process?" I read it over. I still couldn't find it.

You have probably heard the saying: "Seek and you shall find." These words explain how the effort of seeking, and the act of opening your heart, sets up the environment or causation for the "finding" to occur.

"Nature abhors a vacuum," is a law of physics that corresponds to this natural law of life wherein open-minded seeking creates the vacuum for spirit to fill, particularly when we know the answer will come.

Two days after I was reading the book, a client at the clinic remarked that the book was interesting, but that the dedication on the inside cover was "the most meaningful part."

To the wondrous spirit within
which recognizes no self-limitations
and gives the gentle nudging to
accept greater freedom in our lives.

The patient said regarding her success at letting go of smoking and coffee drinking: "It was easy. I was ready for greater personal freedom in my life, and nothing was going to get in the way! Sure, I had headaches for three days, but that's where the nutrition/therapy helped tremendously. Now, I have more energy, look better—people at work have commented—and have more money to spend on coming here and really doing something good for myself."

The message from her comments here—the one that was hidden between the lines in the earlier edition—is that ultimately addictions are a SPIRITUAL issue. Anything that limits personal growth is spiritually limiting and thus a spiritual issue. Life in this world is a continuum of spiritual issues.

Sure, addictions are also connected to not being loved as a child, to resentments, anger, biochemical imbalances, to genetic endorphin shortages, allergic patterns, to the need for energy, and they are intimately related to the different ways to cope with stress in our unnatural, fast-paced environment. But how can these NOT be spiritual issues as well? These conditions are our lessons to learn and our limitations to overcome. Ultimately, we choose our situations and the methods to cope with them.

THE HOLISTIC MODEL

When we look at holistic health we need to consider several points. First, the key to understanding any living organism is that the whole is greater than the parts. Health is representational of a person's diet, environment, and attitude and cannot be abstracted into components of biological machinery.

Second, health is more than the absence of disease. Rather, health is wellness in every aspect of human endeavor. Personal growth, particularly emotional, personal, and spiritual development, is a cornerstone of the dynamics of life and health.

Third, we are responsible for our level of health. Consequently, we are ultimately responsible for any dis-eases that we experience.

Fourth, an understanding of the body's energy more so than its matter is the key for optimal health. The dynamics of quantum physics and the synergism created by quantum chemistry give valuable insights into health and health maintenance.

Finally, natural methods of restoring and maintaining health are preferable to chemical drugs and surgery. Foods, herbs, and homeopathics are based on living blueprints and are compatible with the living body as a whole system. These natural substances most often work in concert with the body rather than poisoning it while suppressing symptoms as chemical drugs do.

If we look at an individual by means of the holistic approach, a human being is a series of wave lengths that can be catalogued as follows:

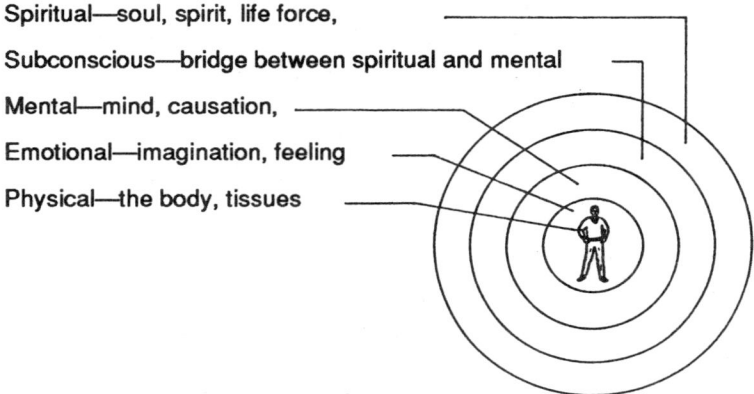

Spiritual—soul, spirit, life force,

Subconscious—bridge between spiritual and mental

Mental—mind, causation,

Emotional—imagination, feeling

Physical—the body, tissues

These different layers interact and make up the whole person.

The addictive patterns can originate on any of the inner, or bottom, four levels. Too much copper in the tissues, or a lack of magnesium or vitamin E, can cause a chocolate addiction at the physical level. A child, who is angered or hurt by a lack of communication with a parent can grow up suppressing the emotional pain with alcohol. A person's mindset to succeed and beat others in business can cause a mental addiction to work. A negative "tape" implanted into a child's subconscious mind—"You can't do this, you can't do that"—can cause a negative self-image that reinforces itself with addictive or codependent relationships or activities.

Whether the focus is nutrition, counseling, or energy work like acupuncture or chiropractic, the role of the holistic practitioner is to show the patient how to resolve the addiction at the proper level. Ultimately, all energy levels must be cleared, right up to the bioenergetic pattern which is the archetypal blueprint out of which a person's life is manifested.

For example, a self-limiting subconscious "tape," such as "I'm not worthy," manifests itself as a mind-set of "I'm not good enough;" which then manifests itself as emotional dissatisfaction and depression; which then manifests itself as physical fatigue, alcohol use, and failure to get ahead financially.

A holistic treatment must provide a way for the patient to reprogram the subconscious tape to, "I am worthy," and a mental attitude that affirms, "I'm the one for the job." A treatment that is holistic must help a person achieve an emotional sense that "it feels great to be successful and happy." The treatment must provide enough physical energy and nutrients to rebalance the body chemistry. This can be done by making up nutritional deficits using supplementation and diet.

THERAPY FROM THE TOP DOWN

If we look at addictions from the top down, from the bioenergetic perspective, we find that a bioenergetic aberration at the subconscious level—whether it be an unworthy self image or a so-called heredity issue—alters the smooth wave form of the individual's energetic pattern. As the wave form interacts with each succeeding level, that level manifests a less-than-optimal picture and passes it on to the next successive level.

An analogy to this in electronics could be that pure high voltage electricity passes through a transformer, and is stepped down for use at a sub-station. But the transforming is less than efficient, and the amperage and cycles are warped. Then the electricity is distributed through another slightly flawed transformer for use in 220 V equipment. And then it is transformed again down to 110 V for use with regular appliances. Then that electricity is run through another less than optimal transformer which is so small that 6 Volt appliances, such as rechargable toys or telephones, can work.

The pure high voltage electricity was flawless, but the first transformer had a warp inherent in it, so the electricity coming out of it was at less than optimal, or aberrant, in amperage and cycles. The flawed electricity is passed along, picking up other flaws each time it is transformed, or stepped down, to another level.

Wave form	Voltage	Analogy
～＼＿／～	flawless wave form	spiritual
～～～～	substation transformer	subconscious
wwwwww	220 V	mental/causal
eeeeeee	110 V	emotional
～～～～	6 V	physical

In looking at addictions from the top down, the question is: Where is the flaw? Is it a poor self image? A poor thought process? An emotional flaw? Or is it a physical problem? The holistic philosophy is to provide support to the topmost and subsequent levels of involvement, and to let the effects transform down to physical success, the arena where we measure most often our success.

We can use an example from homeopathy, the healing science based on the principle of "like cures like suffering," founded by Dr. Samuel Hahnemann. Such classical homeopathy treatment might stimulate the healing force to correct, or adjust, a flaw in the subconscious level by using a perfectly attuned, high potency, constitutional remedy. Then, if that correction can work its way down without subsequent transformers altering it, the person will experience a profound and complete physical healing of the symptoms. If there is any blockage in the healing force's pathway—like another flawed transformer—then an aggravation will occur, giving the homeopath a new set of symptoms upon which to base an adjusting remedy. The fine-tuning of remedies can go on for years, because there may be many symptoms, and many remedies, and multitudes of potencies, dosages, and frequencies of administering doses.

Nevertheless, homeopathy which is the foremost bioenergetic therapy, is an excellent healing system when applied by a capable practitioner. Remedies are non-toxic, nonsuppressive, generally safe, and an excellent alternative to toxic drug therapy. The resurgence today in America of homeopathy because of increasing demands by people is a blessing.

Unfortunately, at the time of this edit in mid 1990, the American Medical Association (A.M.A.) is actively persecuting its members who wish to pursue studies and practice of bioenergetic medicines, such as homeopathy and herbology. This movement to deny the U.S. people safe, effective, and inexpensive healing modalities extends even beyond the boundaries of the A.M.A. membership. Money is funnelled to outside organizations (the Dietician Associations, for example) to limit and make illegal the practice of nutrition, homeopathy, and herbology, except by persons practicing under the jurisdiction of the A.M.A membership—although the members are forbidden to practice these alternative health systems.

The Systemic Health Concept, pioneered by the Systemic Clinic in Austin, Texas, adheres to the bioenergetic principle of providing support to the topmost level of involvement, and to support holistically each subsequent level as well.

The following is a remarkable example for the effects of such holistic treatment. A 7-year old patient—demineralized, with poor digestion, underweight, craving sugar, intellectually very bright, insecure, chronically asthmatic, and stressed—undertook the Systemic Health program. The homeopathic remedy, Silicea 10M, was recommended as the constitutional support. Counseling helped with several deep-seated issues regarding overbearing parents and a need for acceptance. Systemic herbology provided supplements to help the body improve its digestive and enzymatic abilities, adjust the acid/alkaline balance of pH, strengthen the weak adrenal glands, detoxify the reactive bronchial tissue, stabilize blood sugar levels, and improve carbohydrate use. Within two months, the child had noticeable weight gain (9 lbs.), and had only one asthma attack. This attack occurred in the clinic and was brought under control in fifteen minutes with homeopathy and a supplement to balance pH. Six months later, the child's condition was stable: no further asthma attacks, good appetite, and continued good health.

In this treatment program, many levels of the child's health were addressed, and that brought fast, thorough, and effective help. The therapies simply assisted the body's natural healing processes.

THERAPY FROM THE BOTTOM UP

There is another way in which the bioenergetic pattern is affected, giving rise to dis-ease. This way is the one that we are most familiar with: it comes from the bottom up. This bottom-up way shows how our physical activities affect us emotionally and mentally. For example, a sugar binge on sodas and candy can cause emotional weepiness, mental depression, and a host of other symptoms, including lethargy, paranoia, insecurity, and the desire to hurt others.

Unbalancing the emotions and mind can result in new issues such as depression, which can cause a weakened immune system, and thus a flu takes hold. Few people trace the flu back to an episode of anger or depression, or trace the anger and depression back to the sugar binge, or the sugar binge back to whatever set it up.

Many problems represent a "chicken-or-the-egg" situation. Which came first? For this reason, the Systemic Health Concept recommends working on all energy levels simultaneously, or in a specified sequence comprising a therapeutic program.

The following chart demonstrates how it is possible that different addictive substances can disrupt a person's bioenergy on more than one level—from the bottom up. This is only an example of one possibility and does not represent absolute values for the substances examined. Everybody has their own individual values or depth of penetration for each substance listed. This means for example that chocolate can be a giant issue for one person and no issue at all for another.

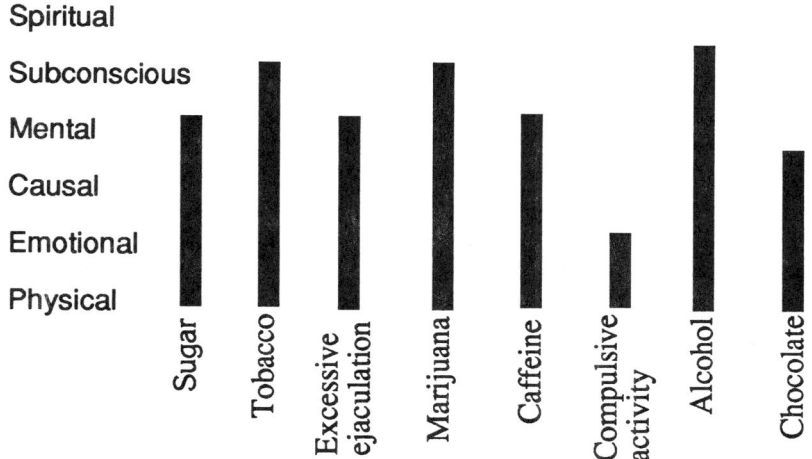

It is not successful to work on emotional addiction at the physical level, but physical level support can greatly help the emotional work. The old adage: "As above, so below," is also somewhat reciprocal: "As below, so above." Therefore the Systemic Health Concept therapy program works from the top down and the bottom up simultaneously.

CLINICAL CASE HISTORIES: FROM THE TOP DOWN AND THE BOTTOM UP

Top Down Example. The patient was a middle-aged woman, divorced, with severe biochemical imbalances revealed by SMAC-25 blood test and hair/tissue analysis. She was addicted to sugar in ice cream. For two months, she participated in comprehensive nutrition work, including full-spectrum nutritional supplementation and herbs to support the liver, pancreas, and adrenals. She waged many a brave battle to delete sugar, but consistently failed. After three months, she admitted her secret, daily marijuana use, which explained the bouts of low blood sugar and the craving for ice cream. After a two-week program to help break the marijuana addiction, she admitted that "it was impossible." At this point she had spent $800 on supplements, lab tests, and consulting services, and while supporting her health to some degree, was not getting much closer to her goal of well-being.

I recommended counseling, upon which the lady reported that she had already spent $3200 with a therapist and was not interested. I pointed out that since she was unable, or unwilling, to follow my counsel, the best I could do was tell her that I loved her in good will and would support her in her health endeavors by recommending a maintenance program.

A week later, of her own volition, she scheduled the recommended session, just to see what it was like. She later reported that during the session it became apparent that she was blaming herself for a divorce, and that she felt unloved and insecure about being alone.

Emerging from the session with a newly found, positive self-image, she was able to let the marijuana habit drop away since it was no longer needed. Having broken the pattern at the emotional level, she replaced it with a new image of her purpose in life. Now she was ready and able to correct the biochemical imbalances that were turning her hair prematurely grey, and to repair the damage of marijuana use: coarse lung tissue, brain impairment, post nasal drip, adrenal fatigue, hypoglycemia. She had to rebuild her health from the ground up. Four months later, she was ready for anything, including her maintenance program. Her new hair growth showed no signs of grey. Ice cream was not such an important issue. "I can take it or leave it," was her comment.

Most addictive activities have their roots in the deeper layers of a person's being. Sometimes, biochemical imbalance is the primary cause, but most of the time it is not. The health practitioner must work with the area of greatest stress, or refer the patient to someone who can.

For example, when necessary the Systemic Clinic refers people to appropriate health care practitioners including medical doctors, dentists, colon hygienists, acupuncturists, massage therapists, psychotherapists, and chiropractors. These other professionals understand the role of the clinic's therapies. The guiding rule is: "What's best for the patient."

Bottom Up Example. While on the subject of ice cream, here is another clinical case history that exemplifies the biochemical approach to ending an addiction. The patient was a 26-year old man with chronic sinusitis, a purulent discharge. He had used massive doses of vitamin C for an extended period of over seven years. Biokinesiology and electro-acupuncture tests revealed that the greatest areas of stress were the colon, the left lobe of the liver, and, of course, the sinuses. The hair/tissue analysis revealed low copper, sodium, and potassium ratios. Urinalysis revealed acid pH and indican, which is a component of urine that reveals the body's inability to digest and process proteins.

The first program was a colon cleanse in combination with the Pro-Vita! Diet. The second program was the Liver Triad with herbs to help the left liver lobe cleanse itself. Information on cleansing the body via the liver is contained in the book, *The Liver Triad* (Tips, 1989). The third program was a continuation of the Liver Triad with the addition of three homeopathic remedies: Kali Bichromium, Silicea, and Pyrogenium all in low potency. The results were quite rewarding, especially for the sinuses. But after two months the patient phoned saying: "I can't make the break from chocolate ice cream. I'm afraid it's going to undo all our work. What can I do?"

"Switch to natural sorbet," I replied. Four days later he called again: "It's got to be chocolate ice cream."

The next day we changed the program to herb based adrenal support, vegetable source vitamin E, and copper supplementation with balanced mineral support. Within two days the craving was gone. We continued nutritional support for two more months, then repeated the hair/tissue analysis. Sodium and potassium were higher and better ratioed, and copper had risen and was better ratioed to iron and other minerals.

The analysis of this case: I suspect that the high levels of vitamin C, which the client had been taking over the past seven years, had depleted his copper levels. Therefore, the primary problem was low copper levels and tired adrenal glands. The years of eating chocolate ice cream had been an attempt to replenish the copper, because chocolate is rich in copper. And eating ice cream had also been an attempt to provide energy, in the form of sugar, to compensate for the tired adrenals. The fact that sorbet did not solve the ice cream dilemma indicated that chocolate, not just sugar, or a milk allergy, were the issue. The ice cream gummed up the colon. And the poor combination of sugar and protein in the ice cream as well as the myriad toxic chemicals, found in commercial ice cream, affected the left liver lobe, thus triggering a sensitivity that reinforced the addictive pattern. The sinusitis was the body's way of getting rid of the toxins through the nose as mucoid matter. These were the toxins which the colon and liver could not handle.

In this case, there was primarily a physical problem that quite possibly was brought on by daily doses of 20 grams of vitamin C, beginning at age 19. Too much of a good thing disturbed the biochemical balance, and poor health was the result.

We have reviewed examples of an emotionally-based and a physically-based addictive pattern, and how the therapies must fit the individual if they are to work.

3

ENERGY ADDICTIONS ARE ENERGY IMPOSTORS

THE HEALTH TRIAD

In this chapter we will discuss why addictions occur. We will also take a look at two types of addictions, and the tools for treatment which lead to and obtaining freedom from addictions.

Chances are great that you have some type of addiction in your life, even though you may not be acutely aware of it. Most people do. And if you do, it is likely that your addiction may have a significant impact on your health and thus limits your chances for a long and healthy life.

If a person is free of all physically addictive substances and activities, then the principles we are discussing can apply to addictive mind-sets. These can consist of fear, guilt, compromises to attain love, codependency, escape from reality addiction (hooked on TV, fantasy, books, etc.), and low self-esteem all of which reinforce the illusion to live a less than optimal life.

In this book we are taking a new look at behaviors and substances that have addictive qualities. We will see how they affect the body's energy system, our health, and the very quality of life.

This innovative information presents a key to nutritional health that can supply everything people want in life, whether it is spiritual, mental, emotional, social, sexual, or physical. This health is based on bioenergy, the vital force of life, which is the basis for all true healing and rejuvenating systems. It is the common thread that unites all healing modalities.

When the body's energy systems work right, you can experience that dynamic, vital, electrically-charged crispness known as abundant health. Nutritionists know that proper physical energy is based on a triad that includes attitude, diet/nutrition, and structure/exercise. This triad must be balanced so that all body systems work together in harmony.

The following illustration of THE HEALTH TRIAD portrays what is a profound secret of health and longevity. Few people, however, understand its implications in their own lives. And, each angle of this triangle is a study in itself. All of the angles are ultimately based on energy. Since our subsequent discussion deals with energy and addictions, it is vital to comprehend this triad concept.

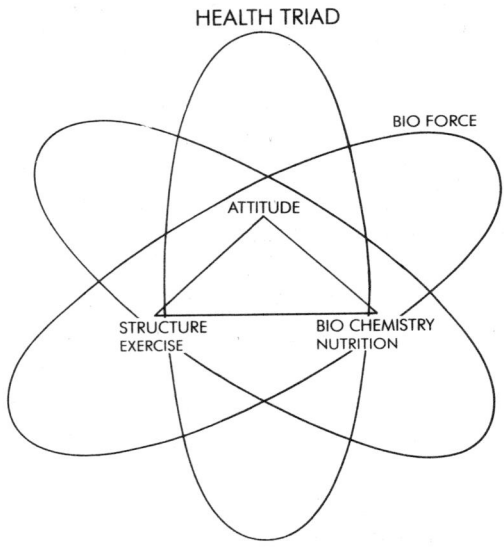

HEALTH TRIAD

BIO FORCE

ATTITUDE

STRUCTURE
EXERCISE

BIO CHEMISTRY
NUTRITION

We will shortly discuss the philosophy of the body's life-energy, its bioenergy, that will form the basis for defining the relationship between addictions and energy. But first, we will establish a working definition of addiction from the perspective of bioenergy. This bioenergetic perspective is more extensive than other ways of looking at the body such as biochemically, pathologically, physiologically, or electrically, because bioenergy encompasses aspects of all of these systems and more.

WHY ARE THERE ADDICTIONS?

Before defining the two major types of addictions, there is a basic question we must ask and understand: why is the human body and human spirit susceptible to addictions in the first place?

Although this is a fundamental question, I have never found it asked before. It seems that we all just blindly accept addictions as a phenomenon of life without questioning their origin. "Yep, addictions can happen. They happen just because they can," seems to be our general, tacit agreement with reality.

Of course, it is quite true that you can take a healthy individual, and against his will inject him with heroin and soon have him addicted. In fact, the designer drug crack can have a person fully addicted after only one experience. This is a plain, physiological fact of life. There are powerful drugs which destroy certain biochemical enzyme functions, and replace them with the perpetual need for the drug. Steroids, such as cortisone for example, often cause an addiction; so do alcohol and cocaine.

But when the original blueprint for life in a human body was set up, why does the possibility for addictions exist in the first place? The fact is that our bodies CAN become addicted.

Drugs, such as alcohol and cocaine, can cause addictions because they can destroy the brain's neurotransmitters (enkephalins, endorphins) which produce feelings of well-being in the brain. The drugs substitute themselves as impostor transmitters while increasing the number of unfulfilled receptor sites. Thus they become the only source which can solve the resulting depression or craving.

Philosophically, addictions exist to hold us back in our personal, spiritual development. They keep life as we know it to be just that...Life as we know it! Free of unexpected occurances, lacking in change and growth. Addictions bind our attention and efforts to their low level. For example, when a nicotine fit occurs, the person can only think about obtaining tocacco.

We often see our addictions as holding on to us — but it is we ourselves who hold on to our addictions.

33

TWO TYPES OF ADDICTIONS: PAIN RELIEF AND PSEUDO ENERGY

To understand the reason behind addictions more completely, we need to gain an understanding of the two types of addictions. Basically, there are two areas of human endeavor involved with addictions: 1) PAIN RELIEF, and 2) obtaining PSEUDO ENERGY. Pain relief deals with the area of neurotransmitters or brain chemicals; energy deals with increased metabolic processes.

Addictive substances and activities fall into either of these categories or a mixture of both. Examples of addictive substances for pain relief include opium and its variations heroin and morphine; anesthetic drugs such as dimerol, cocaine, and so forth. Alcohol can be a pain reliever. But it also can fall into the energy category of addictions, because the bodies of alcoholics actually adapt to run on the energy of metabolized alcohol (carbohydrate). Even a percentage of the tobacco addiction is involved with pain relief, since nicotine functions as a stimulus barrier in the brain and reduces nerve, or pain, impulses being received by the brain.

Examples of pseudo energy-based addictive substances include methamphetamine or speed, sugar, caffeine, tobacco (nicotine), and quite a few others. These substances shift the body into an overdrive condition of high energy and a fast metabolic rate.

To continue looking at the fact that addictions exist to provide for pain or pseudo energy, let's look at two related issues: 1) Why do some people have pain that is unresolved, and 2) Why do some people not have enough energy? (We are aware that another category of severe, chemically induced addictions or deficiencies exist, for example, those induced by powerful drugs like dimerol, cortisone, or heroin. But we are not addressing these types of addictions here.)

PAIN RELIEF ADDICTIONS

The topic of pain relief addictions bears special attention here because it is involved with our philosophy of addictions, or the "why" of addictions. We discussed the physiological process of addictions, pointing out that certain chemicals can profoundly disrupt our biological life processes. It is also known that the oscillations of certain chemicals can profoundly disrupt our bioenergetic processes. A quick example is laughing gas, an inert gas that serves as an anesthetic.

Pain relief addictive substances alter brain chemistry and establish themselves as the impostor for normal brain chemistry. This is discussed thoroughly in the sections on alcohol and cocaine.

But this discussion so far relates to pain at the physical level. What about EMOTIONAL PAIN? It is common practice for people encountering emotional pain to quell the pain with alcohol and drugs. The radio airwaves are filled with songs teaching us that the way to deal with the pain of "she done me wrong" is to "just sit here and drink."

In fact, many people claim that alcohol helped them through the heartbreak of their spouse playing around, divorce, or death of a loved one. But little do these people realize that the drowning of their sorrow literally stifles their proper and healthful processing of the pain. What we are saying here is that alcohol and drugs, used to quell the emotional pain, actually retard the growth and transformation process which such emotional experiences can provide. Drugs often make the emotional pain last longer, sometimes for a lifetime, which is the price paid for reducing the emotion's intensity.

Unprocessed grief is likened to a bacteria which is mutated and pushed in deeper by an antibiotic. For more information on this analogy see the book, *Conquer Candida* (Tips, 1989). Unprocessed emotional pain lays dormant, hidden, smoldering, elusive, poisoning the system, and paving the way for future problems. Ultimately, unprocessed grief sows seeds of destruction by creating the need for further solace from addictive activities. Sweeping grief under the carpet of alcohol or cocaine does not create a clean, joyous life.

Yet, there is an even more profound type of pain that we all deal with, though few people are conscious of it. It is the pain of life in a physical body. The outward focus of our lives through our physical bodies creates an illusion that we are separate from our spirit or soul. Separation is pain, longing, discontent. Generally, people have become estranged from their spiritual nature. This creates a loneliness and fear of death which haunts and disturbs people. The condition represents an innate thought that, "something's missing," or the question, "what's the meaning of life?" The modern estrangement from the spiritual aspect of the human existence causes melancholy and the tendency to seek solace in addictive activities.

ENERGY ADDICTIONS

To obtain a working definition of energy addictions, we need to understand that they are, in effect, addictions to a form of energy. Even the biochemical scenario of the addictive process is based on energy. The chemical reactions in the brain are pathways for neurological, electrical activity. Such ENERGY ADDICTIONS are behaviors and substances that provide a form of energy marked by three characteristics:

1. Energy addictions provide an initial stimulation to the body. But ultimately, they take more energy than they give, and therefore require repetition. Note that sedatives and euphorics inhibit nerve communication, or act as neurotransmitters—endorphins/enkephalins—in the brain. Although users report initial stimulation as the drug takes effect, they actually experience the opposite of energy, namely sedation, relaxation, and a feeling of escape. Some addictive drugs may not fit the stimulation criterion, so we do not classify them as "energy addictions." Instead, these drugs give relief from pain. For example, morphine is a pain killer, or suppressor, and an addictive substance, but it does not usually provide physical energy. Its abuse is not for energy, but for pain relief and escape.

2. Energy addictions provide some form of emotional gratification, solace, or sensory stimulation-sedation. And, people are willing to sacrifice for their addictions.

3. Over time, energy addictions result in degenerative diseases because they weaken the body's endocrine, car-

diovascular, nervous, hepatic (liver), and respiratory systems.

We need to understand that addictive substances are more than chemicals. Yes, such substances are chemicals that have an impact on the body's physical energy system and neurological function, but they are also resonant structures that have an impact on the body's bioenergetic system.

Biochemists can show how the alkaloids in foods or drugs effect the body by their chemical action. From this chemical perspective it is difficult to understand how some substances and activities provide energy when their chemical action depletes energy, as happens with alcohol and marijuana. Some people are so exhausted energy-wise, that they need stimulation to relax. Others are so overstimulated that they need an alternate energy source to balance and relax. Both sides of the energy picture are out of balance and lead to serious health problems.

Because of the bioenergy perspective we refer to addictive activities as a form of energy, or pseudo energy, in this book.

Perhaps the best illustration that energy affects the body as much as chemistry is the anesthetic nitrous oxide, or laughing gas. Laughing gas is considered inert because it does not cause a chemical reaction. Even though there is not a chemical reaction in the body, the laughing gas very effectively puts people to sleep. In effect, the energy oscillations of nitrous oxide cause the dramatic change of putting people to sleep. According to the chemistry textbooks the gas is inert, yet it causes a reaction just the same.

Probably it is easier to understand that energy is the basis for all human activities if we consider that everything consists of energy. Every rock, plant, and living creature is composed of atoms, which represent organized patterns of energy.

We are energy patterns. Nutritionists teach that we live and die at the cellular level. Therefore, our cellular energy, consisting of barely measurable electrical patterns, is the proving ground of our health. These energy patterns are the key to proper cellular function and govern what nutrient material is accepted by the body, and what by-products are eliminated from it.

Several different types of energy comprise a human being: the life-force energy, magnetic energy, electrical energy, meridian energy, and elemental energy. A basic premise about energy as it relates to health is that a human being's primary energy source is within. Energy derives from the body's internal battery, which is able to draw its current from the life force. This is the fundamental difference between the living and the dead states.

In this material we examine activities that provide an artificial physical energy as well as disrupt the bioenergetic pattern of the human being. Such activities are called energy addictions. We now know that addictive behaviors and substances provide a form of energy by stimulating the body in some way. This is stimulation to ignite more energy, or to release or replace endorphins, or to provide stimuli barriers. Nevertheless, these activities or substances end up hurting the body's health in the long run.

Addictive energy sources become necessary when a person is cut off from the flow originating from the internal energy source. The Japanese call this energy-impaired state "sanpaku." And they point out that practically everyone has some of this condition in their lives. In other words, everyone has self-destructive tendencies as well as a survival instinct. Any blockage or imbalance in free-flowing life energies will create the desire for an alternate energy source. People intuitively know when there is an energy imbalance. But instead of confronting or understanding the deep issues, they turn to readily available substitutions, such as sugar, caffeine, alcohol, tobacco, or other drugs.

THERAPIES FOR EVERY LEVEL

This discussion relates to the two types of addictions. We find that some people have bioenergetic and biochemical deficits which are temporarily relieved by addictive substances. Such deficits in the bioenergetic system can best be met more profoundly by bioenergetic therapies, such as homeopathy, acupuncture or systemic herbology, for example. In a biological system such as the human body, bioenergetic deficits can be adjusted most effectively by biological medicines and foods (homeopathics, herbs, vitamins, minerals, amino acids, enzymes).

Admittedly, there are other circumstances involved in addictions. For example, heredity, depression, and allergies complicate the picture of addictive behavior. Nevertheless, we are developing a philosophy about addictions which leaves little room for artificial stimulation of the body and the body's energies by chemical drugs. Instead, we recommend natural, holistic treatments.

Indulging in addictions seems necessary for some people for a variety of reasons. An imbalance in any one of the health triad components—either attitude, diet, or exercise/structure—encourages addiction. Here are a few examples. Poor attitudes, such as self-pity and anger, short-circuit the life-energy flow, inhibit digestion and elimination, and create a need for alternative energy sources. Poor diet causes nutritional imbalances and the desire for a quick energy fix. A lack of exercise allows toxins to accumulate in the cells and intracellular matrix which interferes with the cellular energy, causing the need for an energy source that by-passes the standard body processes (Kreb's cycle of oxidizing acetic acid). Impinged nerves from misaligned vertebrae disrupt the electrical energy supply to vital organs and glands.

An important question concerning addictions, often avoided, is: "What do the heroin addict and the incessant coffee drinker have in common?" Few people want to admit that the same physiological, emotional, and mental pattern accounts for both addictive activities. Whether it is cocaine, caffeine, nicotine, sugar, or any number of other addictions, the common bioenergetic thread makes them all the same symptom; only the degree of damage, the area affected, and the duration of the addiction varies. This means that some addictions are less damaging than others. But why settle for partial health when optimal health is our birthright!

We could establish a scale of addictive substances and activities from least to most harmful, but the scale is different for each individual. Obviously, the hard drugs crack, cocaine, heroin, and speed would occupy the most harmful category of the scale. At the lower end, caffeine can be relatively minor for one person, yet cause the need for a mastectomy or hysterectomy in another person. The elective poisons at the low end of the scale can be small issues with some people, and major issues with other persons. In a worst-case scenario, sugar can be as damaging as speed to a hyperactive child.

Understanding that all addictions are similar and have a common thread can help determine which natural therapies are most likely to help. The addicted person might need to use therapeutic combinations of counseling, herbs, acupuncture, chiropractic, massage, electro-acupuncture, homeopathy, nutrition, and others. We are fortunate that alternative healing methods are increasingly effective. And the tools, such as herbal combinations, homeopathics, and nutritional supplements, are becoming more effective and better guided. A new era in natural healing is well underway, since bioenergy is now increasingly being recognized by the medical and alternative healing professions.

The tendency to seek solace and relief in addictive activities can be helped bioenergetically and biochemically. On the bioenergetic front, Dr. Edward Bach brought forth his healing system known as the Bach Flower Essences. The remedy "Agrimony," for example, has helped many people with addictive behavior.

Stuart Wheelwright also was sensitive to the needs of people caught in a negative feedback loop within themselves which caused a tendency to self-destructive attitudes and habits. Because of his awareness of such conditions, Wheelright incorporated energetic factors into his famous Tai Ra Chi and GOLD herbal formulas to inhibit these detrimental faculties. Many people have reported effective help with addictions when using Wheelwright's formulas.

To summarize our discussion so far, there are pain factors which can establish a tendency to seek solace, and the substances which help relieve the emotional pain can become habit forming. But there are also effective bioenergetic and biochemical formulas to counteract such habits. And there are energy addictions which are effectively treated with bioenergetic and biochemical formulas.

There is another tool that every addictive person needs to understand. This valuable tool is how energy and nutrition relate to addictions. Ultimately, this particular tool paves the way to total freedom from all addictions. It is my desire that this book help point the way to abundant health and greater personal freedom. Therefore we discuss dietary energy in the following section.

BENEFICIAL AND DETRIMENTAL DIETARY ENERGY

The foods we eat can be classified in two categories: beneficial foods and detrimental foods. Some foods are close to neutral, but for the sake of simplicity, we will keep just two categories. The BENEFICIAL foods provide more energy to the body than they require to be digested and processed. In contrast, DETRIMENTAL foods take more energy to digest and process than they supply. Addictive food substances are a subcategory of the detrimental energy foods because they take more energy than they give. Yet, these substances are unique, because they provide pseudo energy so easily, and their detrimental effects are often disguised. For these reasons people often do not realize the damage that detrimental foods ultimately cause.

You might wonder how there could be a negative or detrimental energy substance, or how the body could use it at all. Consider a magnet: both the north and south poles are usable. Either side will stick to the refrigerator and hold a message. Energy is energy.

But the body has its own special energy patterns, therefore outside energy sources with different energy patterns such as foods, radio waves and magnetic fields, will have different levels of compatibility with the body's energy fields. Although detrimental energy sources very effectively stimulate the body, that energy comes with a large price tag, because it is not compatible with the body's life-supporting energy patterns.

We are using the terms beneficial and detrimental energy, instead of positive and negative, because we have a definition problem which should be explained. Magnetically, the negative energy builds the body and the positive energy tears things down. This latter energy, however, is also a valuable magnetic energy. When we refer to diet, the negative polarity is the sustaining energy. Consequently, if we discuss energy as positive (good) and negative (bad) by assigning value judgement terms, we can get into difficulty. For this reason we use instead the terms "beneficial" and "detrimental" rather than positive and negative when referring to dietary energy.

To have a positive or good level of health, the negative magnetic field will help us the most, and that includes beneficial foods, such as whole, organically-grown produce. People can either take in beneficial substances that support the inherent life patterns, or they can consume detrimental substances, which also provide pseudo energy, but do not support the inherent life patterns. It is possible in theory to take in neutral substances that neither give much energy nor take much energy. In reality this is not likely, however, since the body is a dynamic, ever-changing system.

To oversimplify this entire issue of beneficial versus detrimental foods somewhat: when and what you eat, and how it is combined, either supports the body's energy or detracts from it. Information on a bioenergetic approach to nutrition is contained in the book, *The Pro-Vita! Diet* (Tips, 1989). This book is based on the initial research of A. Stuart Wheelwright (one of this century's great herbalists and chemists), combined with clinical insights from day to day practice.

Two factors are the cornerstone of a non-addictive lifestyle and fundamental to breaking energy addictions: 1) a dietary foundation of living foods that support the body's biochemical processes with enzymes, vitamins, minerals, amino acids, lipids, and other nutrient factors; 2) the bioenergetic processes via a compatible, non-disruptive energy field. Diet and herbs can play a remarkable role in changing lives by building the inherent energy within the individual.

And in similar fashion, detrimental dietary patterns and reliance on disruptive, stimulating substances gradually tear down the body and impinge on its free flow of energy, resulting in disease.

The Pro-Vita! Diet explains how you can tailor your diet to build your individual health by balancing both your bio-chemistry and bioenergy. This plan becomes the foundation for a healthy approach to life.

TOOLS FOR LIFE

There are tools, however, that can and should be used for a fuller life. The most important of these is the DESIRE TO CHANGE. This desire, or "engine," can be stoked whenever needed by recognizing that stasis is death, and that change, or growth, represents an essential characteristic of life. Coupled with this strong and sincere desire to change must be the effective use of the CREATIVE IMAGINATION, a powerful and subtle tool that is used to establish a new self-image. As a person's subconscious mind envisions a bright and healthy life through the creative imagination, the seeds for success are sown. Some seeds will fall on the fertile soil of natural health therapies which can provide the nurture needed for change to occur. We discuss imaging and other creative techniques in detail later in this material.

Then must come the FEELING of the new life-style. This must be followed by ACTION, the physical act of stepping aside from addictive behavior and filling the newly created void with something beneficial. Action instead of addictive behavior can include: beneficial and supportive substitutions; just saying "no;" physical exercise; nutritional supplements such as vitamins, minerals, herbs, oils, enzymes, amino acids; homeopathic remedies; exercising a little discipline and a bit of will power; relaxation; using affirmations; and giving service to others which is a quick way to break the "I need" syndrome that is always associated with addictions.

The "I need" syndrome is actually a denial of the unlimited spiritual qualities within each individual. It is an admission and a manifestation of the illusion of "lack." This attitude creates a tacit agreement with reality that "lack" is the operant mode of life that we want for ourselves.

We can all identify with, or at least have known, people who are constantly affirming situations like, "I lack love in my life," or, "Nobody loves me" or, "I need love," or "I sure am lonely," or, "If only somebody loved me then I would feel worthwhile."

Nothing seems to drive love away from a person faster than such attitudes! Holding onto such self-demeaning, self-limiting attitudes is very unappealing. People who are actually potential partners and friends can sense the sad self-image and are turned off. The person who is experiencing a lack of love effectively creates scenarios that reinforce the "I need love" syndrome. And a chocolate bar does wonders for such a wounded psyche by triggering the release or increase of endorphins in the brain. In effect, this endorphine release provides a sense of solace.

When we realize that the only way to get love is to give love, desperate introversion changes into a positive outflow. This is the magnet that attracts love. A person who genuinely loves all life—including plants, animals, and people—has no lack, no shortage of friends and loving relationships.

To apply these insights to the topic of addictions, people who live in a "need" state, who tell themselves things like, "I need a drink," or "I need a cigarette," or "I need a chocolate bar," or "I need to jog a few miles and then I'll feel great," are engaged in addictive behaviors that are ultimately detrimental to health and spirit.

Addictions are a manifestation of, or an attachment to the illusion of fear, which is simply a lack of love. Addiction lowers peoples' self esteem because they silently say, "I give in to the addiction." Many people have found inner strength to abandon addictions by applying the same "giving in" process, but instead of weekly giving in to the addiction, they gallantly say, "I give in to Life, I surrender this addiction to Spirit." In essence, they relax into letting go, then grab for every tool to help the transition.

While discussing the philosophy of addictions, we will look at what it means to be involved with something that creates—we might even say dictates—a demand within us. This discussion reaches beyond physical illness into the spiritual dimension of life.

The basic issue is FREEDOM which is dear to most people's hearts. But freedom is also important to the spirit. When a person relies on substances or behaviors that demand repetition and cause withdrawal symptoms if they are not repeated, a part of that person's being is taken over by that addiction. Something external then rules the person and dictates actions. Addictions make people slaves and limit their experience in such areas of their lives as time, money, creativity, and the ability to enjoy life. Breaking an addictive behavior is a step toward self-mastery and better control over life's circumstances on all levels.

The following is a quote from a testimonial letter that exemplifies the principle that success breeds success:

"Dear Jack:

When I was 20 years old I began daily use of marijuana. I dropped out of college, and subsisted on part-time work and dealing marijuana. Life was fun then. No responsibilities, no cares; "don't worry, be happy," was my motto. One day, after three years of this lifestyle, I realized that the only time I felt alright was when I was high on marijuana. I was dissatisfied with my lack of accomplishment. Also, my health had deteriorated in that I was prone to allergies. By the way, marijuana definitely helped me cope with asthma. As long as I used marijuana I could just barely get by, just barely hang on. So I read your book and decided to get my act together, improve my health, and accomplish something with my life. I re-enrolled in college and got financial aid. Instead of buying books and paying rent, I began a full-out nutritional program and quit marijuana. You told me I must stop immediately, so I gave it all away. That was a big step for me. For the first time in three years, I felt like I could hold my head up. I felt like I had nothing to hide. I didn't feel like the police were my enemies. I liked the way I felt. Your program gave me the support I needed to grab this new direction and not look back. Now, five years later, I'm writing to tell you thanks. Our brief meeting was the turning point in my life. And in just five years, I've graduated with an MBA, have a wife, a daughter, a home, a fine job with a computer company. And here's something particularly important to me, I'm serving my community as an elected official. In other words, where once I was a self-appointed outcast, accomplishing nothing; now I'm productive, happy, and secure in the love of my family and admiration of my community. What a difference! My small success in overcoming what was clearly an addiction to marijuana (although everyone said marijuana wasn't addictive), was simply a stepping stone to other small successes which all add up to a successful, meaningful life. Today closes out a chapter of my life, a five-year plan, and I'm paying homage to those who've helped me become what I am today. I believe that gratitude is absolutely essential to any personal growth, and today I am expressing my gratitude."

At this point we have covered a lot of information, and many concepts have been introduced that are new to you. If any of this material, or the new ideas, are still not clear, do not let that stop you from continuing to read the book. Being introduced to these ideas is the first step toward your understanding of the LAWS OF NATURAL HEALTH. Subsequent chapters will delve deeper into these principles, give more explanations, and include numerous clinical case examples. As you continue to read this information, you will gain a deeper perspective of the bioenergetic functionings of your body. In this way you develop a sensitivity to your own bioenergetic processes.

Since bioenergy is the bottom line for physical health, by reading this book you will soon have the criteria for making decisions which affect your biological health. You will become more aware of the forces affecting your life and find the strength to make positive changes!

4_____

ADDICTIONS: DISEASES OR SYMPTOMS

ADDICTION QUIZ

The discussion in this chapter centers on the question whether addictions are diseases or symptoms produced by underlying bioenergetic aberrations. After providing you the opportunity to take an addiction quiz, you will discover how stress plays into addictions, and how addictions are symptoms rather than disease states.

Addictive substances are impostors. They help to get the job done, that is, they help some people get through the day with some semblance of energy and a minimum of pain. But like a human impostor in a position of power who diverts funds to a private account, addictive energy sources divert the body's energies. In addition, they extract a heavy toll for their services.

Our discussion here is focused on the very substances and activities that for some people seem to make life worth living. We will expose these substances and activities as energy impostors that give us what we seem to need with one hand, while robbing our health with the other hand.

Many of these activities, such as eating sugar or smoking, have become strictly taboo in the eyes of nutritional health leaders. Fortunately, and largely due to the efforts of these nutritionists, the general public is more aware of such health issues.

No doubt, every waitress and waiter who has ever offered dessert to the diners, is aware of the silliness, guilt, and self-recriminating behavior that pops up at that moment. They probably could not count the times when they have heard diners go through the routine: "Dessert? Oh no, I shouldn't—

well, maybe just a small piece." Then, after a few minutes and a flurry of justifications, the customers order large slices of the amaretto chocolate cheese cake. "Well, just this once...."

But guilt, self-recrimination, and a belief in a lack of will power are just secondary effects of an underlying physiological and emotional need. People suffer greatly from self-reproach about the negative nutritional substances they eat. They suffer as well from the emotionally draining behaviors that they take part in. But that is not even the real issue.

The Quigmans

"Frankly . . . we're just too darned WIRED to get anything done."

The point here is that once addictive activities are recognized to be sources of false energy, there is no longer the need to stigmatize those activities by saying "no, no, shame on you," to yourself or to others. Instead, to put it simply, if you do not like the effects of a particular energy source, such as weight gain, nervousness, cancer, diabetes, or expenses, change your energy source from the impostor to the genuine energy. When we have genuine good health, the body is not interested in the energy impostors. Genuine energy is not found in drugs, roasted coffee beans, processed sugar, burning

49

leaves or jogging through the "wall." Genuine energy is born of balanced bioenergetic and biological processes, which in turn are born of positive attitude, whole foods, and proper exercise.

I think that you already have an idea what some of the addictive substances are. But before we go ahead and name them, here is a quick quiz that will help determine whether or not you are relying on unnatural, or impostor, energy sources to help you make it through the day. Circle Y for Yes, and N for No.

Y N Do you compulsively seek activity, push yourself to achieve, feel driven, or obligated, to work harder and harder?

Y N Do you want a little sugar, like candy, desserts, soft drinks or ice cream, in your daily diet?

Y N Do you need or drink coffee, tea or sodas to keep up your energy at work?

Y N Do you love chocolate?

Y N Do you regularly use tobacco or marijuana?

Y N Are there times when LOUD rock 'n' roll music makes you feel better?

Y N Are you a compulsive jogger, meaning that you must jog to feel good?

Y N Do you add salt to your food every meal?

Y N Do you compulsively seek orgasm and ejaculation?

Y N Do you need a drink to relax or use alcohol daily?

A "yes" to any question means that there could be an energy deficit that needs to be satisfied by external stimulation. If you checked all questions with "no," you are either very healthy, very tired, or very boring!!!

Some questions may have surprised you. Before we look at them and at the cause behind these symptoms, we will identify these potentially addictive substances and behaviors.

Potentially addictive substances and behaviors provide a stimulation as adrenaline and/or endorphin release, or a stimulation/neuron-blocking action. These disturbances stimulate the body's energy system artificially. The bottom line is that these substances take away more energy than they give, although people often do not recognize this fact. Potential addictions include: sugar, caffeine, tobacco, alcohol, cocaine, marijuana, compulsive work, jogging, too-frequent ejaculation or need for orgasm, loud rock 'n' roll music, chocolate, and excessive salting of food. More plainly: sugared breakfast cereals, sodas, coffee, pekoe teas, candy bars, cigarettes, chewing tobacco, excessive ejaculation in males, a strong need to jog, workaholic tendencies, beer, wine, mixed drinks, cokes and soft drinks, ice cream, and donuts are all prime candidates for the "potentially addictive hit list."

Note that the focus of this book is not only on socially acceptable behaviors and substances, or elective poisons, but also on some hard drugs, such as cocaine. However, hard drugs like heroin, methamphetamine, and designer drugs will not be discussed in great detail. When people rely on such hard drugs, they enter into a still further degree of addiction which can clinically be called an acute disease. Chronic alcohol abuse also falls into this category, except it is not so acute. Hard drugs disrupt the bioenergy field of the body more swiftly and more deeply than the socially acceptable addictions. Use of hard drugs represents an acute spiritual dilemma that can often end in the sudden fulfillment of the death wish. Lighter addictions work over a period of years and the death wish is realized gradually.

Since we are examining this subject of addictions from a bioenergy perspective as a broader viewpoint, we have included a few behaviors that may have surprised you, like compulsive physical activity, excessive jogging, frantic work schedules, excessive ejaculation and orgasm, and the need to listen to loud rock 'n' roll music to get the body energized. You will soon see how these particular behaviors can fit into the overall addictive pattern.

Most people wage some kind of war against some of the items on the addictive hit list. Their various battles range from gallant attempts at abstinence, to peaceful coexistence, to submissive surrender. Struggling against what seem to be life's little pleasures is one of the many challenges of living in our fast-paced world with its demands on our energy and nutritional reserves.

The stress of hectic lifestyles often leads to the need for quick stress relief, such as cocktails, marijuana, or tobacco, for example. When a drink or a joint helps make things seem all right, it is a symptom that a person's life is too stressed, or the stresses are not being handled effectively. When these actions become a daily necessity, a major adjustment is needed. Some people find that a weekly massage, for example, puts things back into perspective, thus successfully reducing the need for artificial "attitude adjustors."

Now we will discuss briefly the role of stress in addictions.

STRESS AND ADDICTIONS

Since our lives are generally stressful and tiring, people often reach for a quick energy fix, such as coffee, tea, Coca Cola, Pepsi or other soft drink, or a cigarette. Or they need something to calm their nerves, such as a cocktail or joint. To understand how stress and addictions interplay, let's take a closer look at the changes occurring in the body when it is under stress.

Dr. Hans Selye, the famous researcher of the effects of stress on the human body, defined stress as the nonspecific response of the body to any demand made upon it. He named the stress response "the General Adaptation Syndrome" and identified three levels of stress as follows:

- alarm reaction
- resistance
- exhaustion

Selye pointed out that stress was necessary for life and called the complete lack of stress "death." So we learn that stress, as a part of life, is indispensable, but too much stress, or distress, is detrimental to health and the quality of life. When people's lives are such that they experience stress to the point of distress, there is a tendency to exhaustion. And thus we have a condition which can readily be changed by addictive substances.

Normally, a body under stress would go into the alarm stage, then the resistance stage, make a correction, and then return to normal. However, in the presence of continued stress, the body can adapt to a higher level of stress and function accordingly. This gradually weakens the energy system, the thyroid and adrenal glands, and a profound exhaustion can result.

We will take a closer look at this process, because it involves the endocrine system and the body's natural stress response. This is the system that the addictive substances impact. Therefore, understanding the normal process of stress response will provide insights how addictive substances manipulate our bodies.

In the stress response's alarm stage, the hypothalamus gland in the brain signals the pituitary to stimulate the thyroid and adrenal glands, and to secrete the antidiuretic (water retentive) hormone and growth hormone. These hormones from the pituitary, thyroid, and adrenal glands cause many chemical reactions in the body.

The body's metabolic rate increases and causes a higher body temperature. Blood sugar is altered. The cells claim more amino acids. If a ready supply of amino acids is lacking due to a diet that fails to break down proteins or has a dearth of proteins then the body will break down tissue for the protein supply. (Only the Pro-Vita! Diet addresses the proper and adequate availability of amino acids to accommodate stress.)

The additional activity of the adrenal glands causes the thymus gland, the heart of the immune system, and the lymphatic tissues to shrink, thus leaving the body susceptible to infection and illness. At this point in the stress condition, the weak links in a person's health will flare up with symptoms of sinusitis, rheumatism, candida, arthritis, gastritis, colitis, irritable bowel, bronchitis, and so forth.

Then the body enters the resistance stage of stress and attempts to correct the occurring distress. The body's first priority of this second stage resistance is to stop inflammation. The adrenal glands are called upon again, this time to provide cortisol. Cortisol, in addition to quelling inflammation, causes a catabolic or tissue breakdown reaction. Most people recover from stress at this point, or they adapt to it. If adaptation occurs, they enter a stage of chronic deterioration which gradually leads to exhaustion.

Since addictive substances and activities can artificially offset exhaustion and stimulate the adrenal glands, people often perceive sugar, caffeine, nicotine, and alcohol as something that helps them to feel better. These substances help to squeeze a bit more energy out of the energy glands which are already being overworked.

Consequently, instead of returning to a normal state of health, people can endure longer at the exhaustion stage of stress with the help of addictive substances. But this happens, of course, at the cost of pushing the body deeper into exhaustion. For this reason we must avoid the artificial stimulation of caffeine, nicotine, sugar, alcohol, and drugs. Instead, we must return to optimal health after encounters with stress rather than running our health into the ground by demanding performance beyond our inherent abilities.

Effects of the stress response can be measured by the results of the hormonal activity. The effects of hormonal activity include the manipulation (excretion or retention) of minerals, such as potassium, sodium, calcium, magnesium, zinc, iron, manganese, and copper. The excess or lack of a mineral, in relationship to other minerals, gives clear evidence of the stage of stress a person is experiencing. Since minerals are excreted and returned in the hair, an analysis of the hair known as "tissue mineral analysis" or "hair analysis" can provide important insights into what is occurring within the body. For this reason, many nutritionists use the information from a hair test to design nutritional programs for people.

After this discussion how stress and addictive substances interrelate, we address the important topic whether addictions are disease states.

ARE ADDICTIONS REALLY DISEASES?

From one perspective there is evidence showing that addictions closely parallel disease processes. For example, people can have what is called an "hereditary biochemistry" that makes them easily and profoundly addictable to alcohol. This condition of alcoholism is viewed as a disease—the body gone haywire just like a cancer or diabetes. Such conditions may well be treated as actual diseases by therapies that address the causes rather than just the symptoms.

A person, prone to alcoholism, could hereditarily have a low endorphin production in the brain. Inadequate endorphin production causes a deep, all-pervasive depression and the inability to experience joy in living. This depression could be the result of faulty carbohydrate metabolism. Or it could be a functional imbalance of the hypothalamus, pituitary, and adrenal glands due to improper mineral ratios. For some reason, the use of alcohol and sugar, which are both metabolized in the body as carbohydrates, help this person temporarily feel better, perhaps by stimulating an endorphin response or an artificial/imposter endorphin response.

The problems with artificial stimulation are that both alcohol and sugar disrupt the body's bioenergy field, deplete nutrient levels, cause withdrawal symptoms, and promote disease. Alcohol can lead to addiction through the depletion of endorphins. Sugar can lead to a hypoglycemic condition which makes the body dependent on sugar. This hypoglycemic condition can develop eventually into diabetes.

The debilitating effects of refined sugar on the body can be tested easily by using techniques from biokinesiology and applied kinesiology, the sciences of muscle testing. A standard demonstration is to have a person hold a stiff arm against the mild pressure of the practitioner pushing on the client's arm. Initially, the client's arm is strong, showing the person's ability to resist via the deltoid muscle's response. When a packet of sugar is placed on the person's solar plexus (stomach) or parotid gland (jaw under the ear), and the person attempts to hold against the pressure of the test, then the muscle goes weak, and the practitioner easily moves the arm. The person simply cannot hold up to the pressure against the arm, because refined sugar disrupts the body's meridian nerve system virtually universally. The only time this test does not work is when the person "wills" a strong arm and perseveres to keep it strong and fool the practitioner. But in either case the body has to compensate to offset the depleting, bioenergetic influence of refined sugar.

Some people are seriously concerned about the practice of having soda pop machines in schools and hospitals, or the incessant marketing of sugared breakfast cereals to children through Saturday morning cartoons. Are you concerned, too? Some people wonder why dieticians tout the nutritional value of foods that are laced with sugar and preservatives.

But to return to hereditary tendencies—even if a person has an hereditary tendency to addictions, there are answers to be found in nutrition. In fact, many researchers think that up to 95% of all depressive syndromes are metabolic or biochemical imbalances. Depressions are related to addictions since addictive substances can elevate the mood artificially. Therefore it is important to point out that the biochemical imbalances are treatable with nutritional therapies of vitamins, minerals, amino acids, oils/lipids and herbal-glandular supports. These therapies would drastically reduce the per capita intake of antidepressive drugs and their complex and dangerous side effects.

Metabolic imbalances that could cause depression can be revealed quickly by various tests, such as the hair/tissue analysis, the amino acid profile from blood or urine, as well as electro-acupuncture analysis.

The standard, medical SMAC-25 blood test can reveal imbalances which can cause depression. But this test must be interpreted from a nutritional/optimal perspective rather than a pathological perspective, because the body goes to great lengths to keep the blood values normal to retain its homeostasis. Therefore, depressive tendencies are often missed by doctors who do not offer other tests nor interpret the test nutritionally. The leading information regarding the interpretation of the standard blood tests for nutritional information is taught by the American Council of Applied Clinical Nutrition (Clayton, Missouri). Clinicians who are trained and nationally certified in this method present the credentials F.A.C.A.C.N.

Although addictions are considered diseases, it may be dangerous, nevertheless, to think of addictions as such. The disease concept encourages the thought in the afflicted person that "this is something outside myself that is affecting me." Such a notion causes people to surrender their innate ability to be a CAUSE in their own lives. Instead, this thought relegates them to the status of an EFFECT at the mercy of something, or someone, greater than themselves. For some persons, the idea that they are afflicted with a disease often furnishes an excuse to continue in the addiction. They are, after all, in their own thinking "out of control." Others may become brave martyrs trying to overcome a terrible affliction, often failing, but reaping sympathy.

ADDICTIONS ARE SYMPTOMS

Health books are full of research on the topic why addictive substances are harmful to our health and well-being. Researchers cite everything from vitamin deficiencies to carcinogenic ingredients and blame these items as the CAUSE of so many of our diseases. Their insights are not to be denied, but there is another step to take. The nutritional researcher, like an inquisitive child, must approach deep biochemical issues with the childlike question: "Why?" This questioning leads us into a study of bioenergy and nutritional exhaustion.

The basic question is this: IF sugar, caffeine, tobacco, alcohol, and the rest of the hit list items are the cause of such ailments as hyperactivity, cancer, pre-menstrual syndrome, weakened immune systems, hypoglycemia, diabetes, osteoporosis, candidiasis, arthritis, and a thousand other illnesses, WHY do people crave them? Is life so unfair that whatever we like ends up being detrimental to our health, according to all the nutritionists and the more nutritionally oriented medical practitioners?

Not really! It is well known among nutritionists that truly healthy people have no interest in addictive substances or behaviors. And, these people have not given anything up because they honestly have no desire for such substances.

Nutritionists must not stop with a simple list that explains: "These are the bad foods and these are the good foods." If they use such a simplistic approach, they fall into the same trap as the people who accept the antiquated medical model which ignores the body environment by commenting: "Bacteria and virus are bad, but drugs that kill the bad guys are good." The medical model misses the point of asking: "Why did the bacteria and virus proliferate in the first place AND HOW CAN WE PREVENT THE RECURRENCE?" If this question were asked, the discipline of medicine would be studying nutrition and bioenergy, the sciences of the terrain presented in the body.

In a similar way, nutritionists must ask: "Why do people crave detrimental foods?" They must even ask the bold question: "Is that detrimental food really wrong for a person, or is it fulfilling a need in lieu of a better plan?"

For instance, nutritionists know that chocolate weakens the body's energy field, adds toxins to the blood, and affects the liver and adrenal glands. It also affects a person's ability to assimilate nutrients at the cellular level. But we can make a strong case that chocolate could be beneficial for a person with a particular metabolic state and certain mineral imbalances, such as a very high, or very low, copper level in relationship to zinc. The copper inherent in chocolate would then fulfill a necessary, biological need.

No single food is completely good for everyone, even though the marketeers of many health foods would have us believe this. And no single genuine food is completely bad for everyone. Even poisonous plants, such as tobacco, can contain healing attributes. Perhaps the smartest thing a person can do is strive for variety in the diet. That way, the base of nutrients increases, and no single flaw is magnified. This nutritional approach is discussed in the book, *Pro-Vita! Diet* (Tips, 1989), which features a plan for optimal health.

But back to our question: "Why do people crave and enjoy potentially harmful substances?" We can keep the answer simple and honest. People crave such substances because they make people feel good. The substances provide something that keeps people going; they provide a form of energy, a pseudo energy which often appears to alleviate stress. Often linked with that energy is an emotional relief, a momentary solace. Thus, the substances provide something that is missing in peoples' lives.

A telling example concerns chocolate addiction. Chocolate contains a chemical, phenylethylamine, which is the same chemical the brain produces when people "fall in love". These chemicals are associated with the feeling of love. No wonder that chocolates are so appropriate for Valentine's Day gifts! People who need love are frequently attracted to chocolate. But, in effect, craving chocolate is a symptom of a certain type of warp in the inherent bioenergetic pattern.

The same center in the brain which is affected by chocolate is also affected by cocaine and the designer drug XTC. This effect is evidenced by the brief period during which users of cocaine and XTC experience the euphoria of artificially being in love with everyone and everything.

Instead of looking at a hit list of enemies and the myriad diseases they cause, we have now one CAUSE: a lack, or an imbalance, of bioenergy, and its resulting biochemical imbalances. From this discussion we can see that all of the stimulating, addictive activities are mere SYMPTOMS.

We can see that smoking, coffee guzzling, chocolate binges, excessive ejaculation, soda pop fixes, chronic marijuana use, excessive salting of food, and drinking alcohol are mere symptoms of a deficiency in bioenergy. From the bioenergetic perspective we can understand that all of these addiction symptoms are something like a headache, menstrual cramps, runny nose, and all the other socially acceptable afflictions of the human condition.

Let me emphasize for you again: addictions are symptoms of bioenergetic and biochemical imbalances. Addictions are not simply related to poisonous substances that cause ill health. It does not matter whether addictions are hereditary or inborn; depression-based, either nutritional or biochemical; or stress relieving. In order to work with the cause of addictions, we must address the body's subtle energies; its physical energy or endocrine system; its fuel or diet; its wiring or nerves; its endorphins and neurotransmitters; and its battery or minerals and amino acids. It is important to notice how all of these factors revolve around the health triad that we discussed earlier.

Now that we understand that addictions are symptoms, perhaps people will be more compassionate toward themselves and others who need to bolster their energy through addictive activities. We do not need any more "thou shalt nots." Instead, we need to be more understanding of ourselves and others. And it is important to emphasize that the science of holistic nutrition is the science of health and energy. The proper bioenergy system which the body was designed to use, consists of balanced nutrition, enhanced with beneficial attitudes, and positive outflow.

If people could simply acknowledge that the continual need for sodas, for example, is a SYMPTOM, they would be able to take a look at the CAUSE, which is the bioenergy imbalance. Then they would be able to direct a cure, or a return to a more optimal degree of health by choosing bioenergetically supportive therapies.

5

ADDICTIONS DEPLETE THE BODY'S NATURAL ENERGY SYSTEM

THE CAUSAL CHAIN

In the previous chapter we examined the effects of stress on the human body. Since the body's natural energy system is essentially related to the endocrine system, it is important to understand how the two energy glands function. Therefore, this discussion centers on the adrenal and thyroid glands, and how you can test whether they function adequately.

People involved in stress, fatigue, and addictive substances are participating in a causal chain which ultimately breaks down the body's energy and immune system. This chain functions as follows:

1. Stress, through the nervous system, affects the endocrine system of glands and hormones, resulting in fatigue.
2. Addictive substances and activities are often used to counter the effect of stress, resulting in a deeper and more profound disturbance of the bioenergetic and biochemical balance.
3. Stimulated by stress and/or the addictive substances, the endocrine system suppresses the immune system.
4. A chronically depressed immune system leads to chronic, degenerative diseases, while a temporarily suppressed immune system can leave a person susceptable to acute illness.

At the center of this chain are the thyroid and adrenal glands. They play a central role in the body's energy system.

For this reason we present a summary of scientific information on these glands.

THE ENERGY GLANDS: THE THYROID

The THYROID gland is an endocrine gland which produces hormones. The thyroid is located in the front of the neck above the collarbone at approximately C-6 cervical vertebrae level.

The primary hormone produced by the thyroid is Thyroxine which increases oxygen use in virtually all body tissues. Thus the thyroid is a major factor in the metabolic rate of the body. The thyroid also produces a hormone called Calcitonin which inhibits the rendering of calcium from the bones into serum.

The thyroid further produces a hormone, called Parathormone, which is responsible for maintaining proper calcium ion levels in the blood and tissues. It stimulates the disintegration and resorption of bone matter as the primary source of calcium for maintaining the calcium ion (pH buffer) in the blood. Since calcium is critical for heart function, muscle function, blood clotting, and pH control, these tiny glands play a critically important role in health.

The thyroid is considered to be the master METABOLIC REGULATOR. The body's metabolism is the rate at which the body builds up and tears down. A primary issue of metabolism is how fast fuel oxidizes or burns, and how waste products are disposed of at the cellular level. If the thyroid is not functioning correctly, important metabolic change will result.

An underactive thyroid produces hypothyroidism which can result in yellowish skin, puffy mucous layer under the skin (myxedema), fatigue, weight gain and inability to lose weight. For example, FATIGUE is a primary symptom resulting from the lowered rate of living at the cellular level. Hypothyroidism is more widely spread than medical sciences recognizes at this time. Approximately 40% of the American population suffers from low thyroid function, known as "subclinical hypothyroidism". Sufferers do not have blatant thyroid malfunction, but have an illusive, general malaise.

This general malaise is the result of poor protein and sugar use by the body. Protein is the major building block of the tissues. Thyroxine increases protein use throughout the body. In a subclinical hypothyroid condition, the proteins are not effectively delivered to the cells. In children, this results in a lack of development. In adults, this results in poor health and loss of tissue integrity.

The thyroid plays a vital role in nutrition via the utilization of fuel by the body. The process of using protein for fuel—the breakdown of protein into sugar for the proper fuel mix for the body—is called "gluconeogenesis" and is regulated by thyroxine. The breakdown of fat into glucose—also for the proper fuel mix of carbohydrate, amino acid, lipid—is influenced by thyroxine, too. The level of fat in circulation is governed by the thyroid and blood cholesterol levels. Therefore, a low thyroid function means higher cholesterol.

Thyroxine also helps determine how much sugar is absorbed from the gastro-intestinal tract into the body, and the rate at which glucose is burned by the cells. People who have problems with sugar metabolism are well-advised to support the thyroid.

Hyperthyroidism is the condition caused by an overactive thyroid, and consequently there is too much thyroxine in the bloodstream. Symptoms of hyperthyroidism are the opposite of hypothyroidism. The body's metabolism is too fast, the body motor idles too fast. Nervousness, insomnia, increased heart rate, decreased weight, inability to gain weight, poor balance when standing on one leg, thin skin, delicate features, increased appetite, and erratic behavior are all effects of over-activity of the thyroid. In more severe cases, tremors, goiters, and protruding eyeballs occur.

THE ENERGY GLANDS: THE ADRENALS

The two adrenal glands are located on top of the two kidneys (ad = near, renal = kidney). Also called the suprarenal glands (supra = above), these glands are the size of large beans. The adrenals secrete more than fifty vital hormones and similar substances. These hormones, which are steroids, also play a role in the anti-inflammatory response of the body and thus are in a feed-back loop with the immune system. People with allergies and asthma always have weak adrenals. Because the adrenal glands produce so many hormones, they are critically important to the body's metabolic regulation.

The adrenals are actually two different glands encased in one capsule and are differentiated as the adrenal CORTEX and the MEDULA. The CORTEX secretes hormones which help the body regulate its metabolism of amino acids, carbohydrates, electrolytes (minerals which provide electrical chemistry), and water. The hormone aldosterone as well as other mineralocorticoids are secreted as a response to the presence of certain enzymes in the blood. This process helps the body regulate its electrolytes (sodium, potassium) for the electrical function of cellular metabolism. This cellular metabolism represents the body's "spark in the battery."

The hormone cortisol as well as other glucocorticoids are secreted by the cortex to assist with the carbohydrate/energy metabolism. Thus the adrenals are in a "feed-back loop" with the pancreas and are part of the "hypoglycemic cycle" in people who suffer from low blood sugar. The hormone ACTH from the anterior pituitary stimulates the introduction of cortisol into the bloodstream.

The sex hormones, such as estrogen and testosterone, are also produced in small quantities by the adrenals to assist the gonadal (ovaries/testes) production. For this reason some women do not require estrogen replacement therapy after a hysterectomy involving one or both ovaries.

The adrenal MEDULA is "wired" with nerves and produces the hormone epinephrine which is responsible for the "flight or fight" survival response. Epinephrine boosts the metabolic rate and provides for the breakdown and mobilization of carbohydrate (glycogen) and fatty acids (lipids) for immediate energy. This hormone mobilizes blood from the spleen, kidneys, and intestines, and sends it to the brain, muscles, and lungs.

The adrenal connection with the nervous system is important, because a person who worries or mentally imagines frightening or vengeful scenarios causes a stimulation of the adrenals via the sympathetic role of the autonomic nervous system. Embryonically, the adrenal medula was derived from the autonomic nervous system. Because nerves affect the adrenals, tense people run their adrenals down. To help such a case, both the nerves and the adrenals must by supported by nutrition and herbal formulas.

The adrenals are one of the primary pH regulating organs which also includes the lungs, gonads, and kidneys. When the adrenals fail or become exhausted, the urinary pH will lock into an acid range of 4.5-5.5 as a self preservation mechanism. Although the urinary pH is acid, this is actually indicative of a deep alkalosis condition in the body.

Consequently, the small adrenal glands are absolutely essential for life and maximal health. One gland can be removed with little side effect. But if both are removed, death results within a couple of hours. Other than the brain, the adrenals are the body part most richly endowed with blood.

From a bioenergetic perspective the adrenals are part of the "Triple Warmer" or endocrine-sex meridian in acupuncture. The adrenal cortex is yang or masculine. The adrenal medula is yin or feminine. The adrenals are the body's primal brain and take charge when it is confronted with "life and death" situations.

Low adrenal function results in timidity, fear, cowardliness. High adrenal function results in bravado and macho behavior. Proper adrenal function results in physical and mental strength and alertness.

Recreational drugs (amphetamine, cocaine, nicotine, marijuana, caffeine, heroin, etc.) stress the adrenals and can result in "adrenal burn out." People with a history of drug use often have "hollow" or depleted adrenal tissue. When the adrenals are depleted, therapy must be provided to effectively rebuild them.

ADDICTIONS WEAKEN IMMUNITY

Addictive behaviors and substances often provide a temporary lift in energy by stimulating the energy glands, the adrenals and the thyroid. In tum, people whose energy glands are weak have a tendency toward addictive substances, because these substances provide ARTIFICIAL STIMULATION. In essence, such substances provide a pseudo energy source for these persons' bodies. But, like investing money at 7% interest when the inflation rate is 9%, eventually using addictive substances end up on the short side. The short side of cellular energy is disease, caused by a weakened immune system.

Why a weakened immune system as result of using addictive substances? Because the adrenal glands act in opposition to the thymus gland which is one of the major immune system regulators. When the adrenal glands are stimulated and are secreting their high-energy hormones, adrenaline and cortisol, the thymus function in turn is greatly reduced. Therefore immunity to disease is diminished. For this reason, users of addictive substances are often more susceptible to colds, infections, sensitivities or allergies, candidiasis (infection by the yeast/fungus Candida albicans), and other immune-deficient diseases.

Moreover, cortisol, an adrenal cortex hormone, is an important regulator of blood sugar levels. Addictive people inevitably have adrenal insufficiency, which contributes to low blood sugar, fatigue, and sugar cravings.

The adrenal glands have other immune system support roles. If they are weakened, their role and ability to participate in the body's immune response is diminished.

An example of diminished immune response relates to the antifungal, antibacterial, anti-mold mineral copper. With proper adrenal function, this oxygenating mineral is available to the body. When there is adrenal insufficiency, copper is either stored deep in the tissue, where it is unable to do its job, or it is lost (excreted), and the body becomes deficient. Without adequate copper levels, the immune system is weakened. Also, complete recovery from fungus-related diseases is dependent upon the restoration of biochemical balance. This is accomplished through the endocrine glands, pH balance, and nutrition. All of these factors affect the biochemical balance.

If we consider a diminished immune response from a hormonal standpoint, we find that the hypothalamus, pituitary, and adrenals miscommunicate in such a condition. This causes poor carbohydrate metabolism which, in turn, often causes a predisposition to depressions which are temporarily relieved by eating sugar. All of these stages form a complex chain of events that keeps the immune system either overactive or suppressed.

Have you ever known smokers who never catch colds until they quit smoking? In clinical nutrition, we know that when people say they never catch colds they are either very healthy or very sick, actually too sick to respond to colds.

Smoking is an example of an addiction that is lowering the body to a chronic degenerative state rather than an acute illness. In contrast, colds, flu, and acute illness reflect an active, higher-energy state, because the body still has the ability to cleanse itself and weather the discomfort. If the body cannot cleanse itself, then death can result.

If an acute condition gets worse, it becomes chronic, degenerative, and simply smolders. This condition continues until there is either enough energy for the body to reverse the chronic condition into an acute condition and cleanse itself. Or the condition degenerates even further, contributing to the eventual death of the body.

In naturopathy we work to support the natural healing process of the body, rather than suppress the cleansing symptoms, as people often do when they turn to drugs to eliminate a symptom. In fact, the suppression of symptoms often drives the acute cleansing into seemingly unrelated chronic diseases. Therefore, it is better to have a couple of colds a year than to live every moment with a degenerative disease.

If you live close enough to the Health Triad principles, as discussed herein and presented in the book, *The Liver Triad* (Tips, 1989), and if you build your health daily, you will probably not even have the couple of colds a year to endure.

The words "artificial stimulation" were used previously in our discussion, because addictions harness pseudo energy system. It is like running a car around town all day on its turbocharger—just to go to the grocery store. Unnecessary wear and tear.

The following substances or behaviors all cause artificial stimulation which seriously affects the adrenals: nicotine, caffeine, cocaine, sugar, marijuana—a source of the toxic metal cadmium—compulsive exercise, an excessively frequent need for excitement to orgasm (particularly in males), chocolate, alcohol, and excessive salt. All of these stimulate the adrenals to produce hormones such as adrenaline, a hormone normally reserved for fight-or-flight situations. Adrenaline raises blood pressure, accelerates heart rate, causes the liver to release sugar into the bloodstream, and expends a great amount of reserve energy. Constant stimulation can burn out the adrenal glands just like excessive use of a turbocharger can burn out a car's engine. Burned out adrenals result in fatigue and a craving for artificial stimulation. Note that the use of high-sugar items kicks in the adrenal turbocharger at a different level and calls for other adrenal hormones. The result, however, is the same: overstimulation and overwork resulting in a greater energy deficit.

SELF TEST FOR ADRENAL GLAND FUNCTION

The adrenal glands can be underactive, or hypoactive, due to sluggishness, caused by elevated serum calcium, lack of exercise, weak nerves, or stress; or due to exhaustion from working too hard for too long; or from having a history of drug use, overwork, or emotional crises.

The following is a simple test for underactive adrenal function. To perform this test, all you need is a blood pressure gauge, or sphygmometer, to compare two blood pressure readings. These are the three easy steps for the test:

1. Lie on your back and relax for five minutes. Have your blood pressure recorded. We are interested in the systolic reading, which is the first, or higher, reading.
2. Stand up and immediately take your blood pressure again.
3. If the systolic reading does not rise a few points (it should rise 2 to 10 mm), or if it drops, you can suspect underactive, underresponsive adrenals.

The degree of drop, if it occurs, is known as orthostatic hypotension, and it is directly related to the degree of adrenal underactivity.

Symptoms of weak adrenals include fatigue, low stamina, dizziness, headaches, memory weakness, allergies, susceptible constitution, sensitivity to bright light, skin eruptions, dehydration, food cravings, and hypoglycemia.

In our clinical work, we frequently use the test to measure adrenal function. Then we give the client with a low reading a nutritional formula (the Wheelwright Ga formula), containing adrenal protomorphagens, the adrenal triad RNA structure (adrenal/thyroid, pancreas, spleen), bioenergetic factors, and nutrients in a Brazilian herb base. Five minutes later, we repeat the test—most often with astounding improvements! This test can be used to measure the efficacy of the nutritional approach to adrenal support.

SELF TEST FOR THYROID FUNCTION

The test for determining the thyroid function is a simple, fairly accurate, basal-metabolism test. Put a thermometer by your bed, within arm's reach so that you do not have to sit up to reach it. When you wake up, do not get out of bed. Just reach over and place the thermometer in your arm pit for 15 minutes. Do not move around. Record your temperature at the end of 15 minutes. It is best to do this each morning for five days. Temperatures of 97.6 degrees Fahrenheit, or lower, may indicate underactive thyroid function.

Like the adrenal glands, the thyroid gland can be underactive from sluggishness due to lack of circulation, or poor nerve supply; from subluxated cervical vertebrae; from poor nutritional supply of iodine and fatty acids; from lowered pituitary function; or from long periods of overactivity leading to exhaustion.

An underactive thyroid can cause symptoms such as dry skin and hair, fatigue, inability to lose weight, depression, and cold hands and feet. A hair test indicating a high calcium/potassium ratio is indicative of an underactive, or hypoactive, thyroid. And a low ratio accurately predicts an overactive, or hyperactive, thyroid.

A side note here: the thyroid plays an important role in cholesterol levels of the blood. An underactive thyroid leads to elevated cholesterol. This is why thyroid support is important in a program for cholesterol reduction. Yet few clinicians pursue this course and opt instead for the more popular dietary use of oat bran and avoidance of cholesterol foods.

In our clinical work, we have found that a nutritional base of dulse, or kelp, with flax seeds provides the necessary nutritive factors for a healthy thyroid. We also have found that an herbal combination formula, Systemic Gf, featuring the RNA/DNA factors (protomorphagens), the thyroid triad (thyroid, lung, thymus), bioenergetic homeopathics, and a Brazilian herbal base, is particularly effective in improving basal metabolism as well as adjusting cholesterol levels.

Also, light aerobic exercise upon arising and before bed is important to maintain proper basal metabolism. This is particularly important for people who are overweight due to a sluggish thyroid.

The traditional medical blood tests for thyroid function (T-3, T-4, T-7) are notoriously inaccurate indicators of overall thyroid function, since they do not reveal a poor thyroid function until it is quite poor. Fortunately, many doctors are requesting more detailed lab tests, because they are finding hypothyroidism to be a major factor in people's symptom pictures. Few clinicians understand that a high thyroid test score is actually indicative of a low thyroid function, and a low test score indicates a hyper functioning thyroid. This contradicts the currently accepted interpretation that high values represent an overactive thyroid, and low values an underactive thyroid. However, this does not matter in clinical nutrition, because both a hyper and hypo thyroid are treated with the same therapy designed to restore balance in the thyroid function.

Clues regarding thyroid function can also be found in the sclera, the whites of the eyes. A. S. Wheelwright, the modern-day founder of sclerology, the science of interpreting the red lines in the whites of the eyes, has catalogued the various lines that relate to thyroid function. These include congestion, toxic thyroxin, iodine poisoning, radiation poisoning, infection, adhesions, glandular fatigue, and abnormal cells, for example. The following picture is an example of such lines in the sclera:

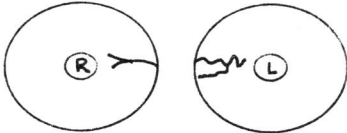

This chart reveals that the right lobe of the thyroid is stressed and overworked, while the left lobe is sluggish and congested. But in the T-3, T-4, T-7 thyroid blood test, this person's thyroid would appear normal. Actually, the right thyroid lobe is compensating for the left. This causes an averaged-out blood test measure, although the overall gland is stressed.

Note: To learn more about sclerology contact the International Sclerology Foundation, Inc., c/o 4001 Manchaca Road, Austin, Texas 78704-6737. Information is available on the manual, charts, tapes, and certification courses.

6

ELECTIVE POISONS

In this chapter we take a closer look at the more common symptoms mentioned previously in the addiction quiz. Other symptoms will be discussed in the following three chapters.

SUGAR

This term refers to refined, simple sugars as found in soft drinks, candies, and other products. These sugars bypass several stages of the natural body processes that convert complex carbohydrates into glucose for energy and thus have a stressful impact. In effect, sugar is a drastic, quick energy fix that ultimately weakens the ability of the pancreas to regulate blood sugar levels through insulin production. For the slow oxidizer (a person whose thyroid and adrenals are underactive), sugar crashes through the pokey metabolism, and provides a shot of energy that is quickly used and unfortunately appreciated, leaving behind nutritional and energy deficits.

Back in the late 1960s, it was in vogue to have hypoglycemia, a condition of low blood sugar based on overconsumption of refined sugars in the diet. The condition was the result of living in an affluent society with an abundance of processed, sugared foods available on the market.

But hypoglycemia is not just a pancreas problem, as many people think. Blood sugar problems also involve the liver, hypothalamus, pituitary, and adrenals. The liver is responsible for the glucose levels of the blood. The hypothalamus regulates the "automatic" body functions. The pituitary gland (anterior lobe) synchronizes hormonal levels. Finally, the adrenals provide a sugar metabolizing hormone, cortisol. Clearly, sugar consumption impacts the entire system by putting a stress on very important metabolic activities.

For in-depth information on the biochemistry of sugar addiction, read *The Hidden Addiction* by Drs. Phelps and Nourse (1986). Their clinical experience has shown that sugar addiction is the world's most widespread addiction, and probably one of the hardest to kick.

Even people avowed to their health often flirt with sugar addiction. Though they shun candy and sodas, they will instead use honey, dates, dried fruit, and fruit juices to provide the energy their systems still lack. These substitutions are preferable to the more detrimental sugars, because the more natural sugars are accompanied by vitamins and minerals rather than containing just empty calories. However, to the body chemistry, sugar is sugar. Pasteurized fruit juices contain very high sugar levels minus the enzymes of fresh juice and can impact the body very similiar to candy and sodas. The use of the more natural sugar substitutes may indicate blood sugar problems with even the more health-oriented diet and an inherently weak energy system.

One reason for this is that in the attempt to eat better, people still neglect the proper intake of low stress proteins which are the balancing factor in metabolic energy. Currently many nutritionists are promoting a complex carbohydrate orientation to diet, but this will not solve the blood sugar problems already created by previous overindulgence in sugar. It only smooths it over. According to our clinical studies, only the Pro-Vita! approach to diet will strengthen the sugar-weakened body systems.

If you require something sweet to feel good or to get going—even that little lift in chewing gum—consider it a symptom of an energy lack, and a warning that it is time to take steps nutritionally. Systemic herbology, which is a comprehensive healing system, recommends simultaneous support of the liver, pancreas, adrenals, pituitary, and hypothalamus. Such therapy has been very effective in helping the body quickly put an end to hypoglycemia, PMS symptoms, and general fatigue. Supplementation, along with the Pro-Vita! Diet, often corrects blood sugar irregularity within two to six weeks. Additional time is required to rebuild the weak systems.

There is broad acceptance of the orthomolecular concept: "When under stress, take additional B-complex vitamins." This is basically a good idea because stress depletes the B vitamins rapidly. But actually, the critical nutrient lost due to stress is minerals. Mineral supplementation is therefore even more important than vitamin supplementation. It is interesting to note that people under stress often crave sugar, when, in fact, sugar is known to deplete B vitamins. It is typical of addictive activities to put the body into an even greater energy and nutritional deficit, thus requiring repetition of the impostor energy source.

Mega doses of B vitamins do not promote a balanced system or cure the effects of stress. In fact, they usually add an additional burden to the body since the liver must process them. It is much more supportive to take a moderate B-complex and sea-based mineral complex to minimize the nutrient toll of stress.

Sugar craving is most often a sign of a lack of nucleoproteins, the amino acids available at the cellular level. This topic is addressed by the book, *Pro-Vita! Diet* (Tips, 1989). The craving of sugar can also be a result of a weakened immune system that has allowed candida yeast or other pathogenic micro organisms to flourish. This situation is covered in detail, with never-before-published clinical data, in the book, *Conquer Candida* (Tips, 1989).

Sugar is like jet fuel for the body and a little bit goes a long way. In the natural order of body function, the body synthesizes its own sugars from carbohydrates, fruit, and other nutrients such as fats and proteins. The body's actual requirement of processed and refined sugars is nil, yet the per capita consumption of sugar in the United States exceeds 115 pounds a year.

The tissue mineral analysis (hair test), based on an assay of a small amount of hair by a reliable lab, is invaluable to determining the proper nutritional steps. Mineral ratios based on minerals being excreted through the hair reveal a great deal about a person's energy system. If a nutritionist can correlate that information bioenergetically, and provide glandular supports as well as biochemical supplements, then dramatic improvement in a person's health can be expected.

Just for fun, can you guess how many teaspoons of sugar are in one can of Pepsi? Go ahead and guess:

_____2 teaspoons, _____ 5 teaspoons, _____ 10 teaspoons?

Many people guess the answer is two teaspoons, but in fact there are ten teaspoons of sugar dissolved in Pepsi.

NUTRASWEET. Nutrasweet is not a viable substitute for sugar from the nutritional perspective. It is neither considered beneficial nor safe for health in nutritional circles, despite the extensive advertising to sell Nutrasweet's wholesomeness to the public, and even though it carries the approval of the FDA.

In fact, the chemical name for Nutrasweet is aspartame which is composed of 50% aspartic acid, 40% phenylalanine, and 10% methyl alcohol (wood alcohol). The chemical makeup contains alcohol, and we know that some people are addicted to alcohol and have alcohol allergies which completely disrupt their brain chemistry.

Moreover, the methyl alcohol in Nutrasweet is highly toxic, so toxic in fact that the body is unable to break it down. The advertisements make claims that methyl alcohol is natural since some fruits contain a trace, but they fail to point out that the fruit alcohol is bonded with ethyl alcohol, a molecule which assists the chemical breakdown of the toxic methyl alcohol. This bond is missing in Nutrasweet.

The Medical Director of the Palm Beach Institute for Medical Research, H.R. Roberts, M.D., has diagnosed hundreds of people suffering side effects from the use of Nutrasweet. These side effects of the methyl alcohol include seizures, headaches, blindness, depression, dizziness, confusion, and disorientation. The people most sensitive to such side effects are babies, children, women during pregnancy, women during lactation, diabetics, hypoglycemics, epileptics, and people who suffer from migraines and allergies. Clearly, Nutrasweet is not safe and is not a viable way to avoid sugar.

I have to admit that it breaks my heart when I see mothers fill their shopping carts with coke and other soft drinks and also put these drinks into their baby's bottles. I have observed people spend $50 worth of food stamps on sodas, potato chips, and candy—all destined for the mouths of their infants and children. How do these kids ever get a chance in life? Sugar soon warps the bioenergetic pattern so that the children lose their taste for wholesome foods. Instead, they desire only carbohydrates and sugar.

But even the health food industry fools trusting shoppers with alternatives to soda pops. In general, natural sodas are an improvement over traditional soft drinks because they do not contain chemicals, preservatives, and caffeine. But many natural sodas are still high in sugar via high fructose corn syrup. Currently, only the soft drink brand Sundance does a fine job of being natural, avoiding the high sugar levels because it does not contain high fructose corn syrup. And the drinks are still very tasty! Fortunately, these sodas are becoming available at supermarkets nationwide. The only question left regarding these natural sodas is the quality of the white grape juice used as a base. Were the grapes grown without pesticides?

Here is another little quiz: Are carob candy bars sold in health food stores much more nutritious than regular chocolate bars? True or False?

As you might have suspected, the answer is "False". Both types of candy bars are detrimental to health because both are loaded with sugar and fat. In addition to some form of sugar, many of the health food candies contain palm kernel oil, coconut oil, or cottonseed oil which are quite devastating to the cardiovascular system. Research has shown that palm and coconut oil contribute to heart disease much more than a hamburger. Cottonseed oil has the same effects, and it probably also contains DDT or other pesticides, used to combat the boll weevil and other cotton crop pests. Since cotton is not considered a food crop, it is not regulated by the same stronger laws that govern foods. Thus the pesticide issue is a major concern with cottonseed oil.

Only careful reading of labels and experimentation can lead you to natural, low sugar treats that do not have an excessively detrimental effect on health and still taste great. It is important that the more natural replacements or substitutions for the harmful treats taste good so that the switch is not a major sacrifice or a settling for second best. Ten years ago this was the case and the health food treats often were less tasty substitutions. Now there are several innovative, healthful products available as substitutes for sugar products.

In summary, lowering sugar consumption improves health. In homeopathy and systemic herbology, a craving or desire for sugar is a symptom of impaired health.

STIMULANT BEVERAGES: COFFEE, TEA, CAFFEINATED SODAS

This section on stimulant beverages refers to caffeine and oxalic acid, two chemicals that stimulate the adrenals, exhaust the liver, and deplete valuable nutrients, such as calcium and zinc. The excessive stimulation by these drinks damages the nerve portion of the adrenals and turns on the adrenaline, the turbocharger.

COFFEE. Oxalic acid in caffeinated as well as decaffeinated coffee gradually destroys the central nervous system. Oils from coffee coat cell membranes, thus blocking the transfer of nutrients through the sodium-potassium exchange and the cell's mitochondria faculty.

Most importantly, roasted coffees contain tars similar to the tars from smoking tobacco. This is a primary issue which also puts decaf coffee on the list containing items less than optimal for health. Caffeine is disruptive to the bioenergetic as well as the biochemical system. The tars from roasted coffee are particularly damaging to the basic biological systems of the nutrient utilization. Therefore, the consumption of coffee is a serious health threat.

It should be noted that decaffeinated coffees still contain oxalic acid, and often contain petrochemicals that are used in the decaf process. Methylene chloride is often used to decaffeinate coffee. It introduces into the body a chlorine-carbon molecule which is identical to the active ingredient in insecticides. Methylene chloride is known to cause cancer. Ethyl acetate is another chemical used to process decaf coffee. Although it is less toxic than methylene chloride, it remains suspect as a petroleum product. Bioenergetic testing shows that ethyl acetate, and products processed with it, are more disruptive in the body than the water-processed decaf brands.

Decafs produced by the dangerous methylene chloride process include Maxwell House, Sanka, Brim and Yuban, all marketed by General Foods. Decaf coffee produced by using ethyl acetate includes Folger's and High Point.

If you use decaf coffee, buy it from your health food store, and choose a brand that does not use petrochemical solvents, but instead uses a water decaffeination process. This is an improvement and avoids the bioenergetic disruption caused by petroleum-based decaf processes.

Water-processed decafs include Taster's Choice, Nescafe, and Maragar Gold.

Coffee reduces the body's tolerance to pain. Chemically speaking, it competes with naloxone for binding to opiate receptors in the brain. Both coffee and decaf coffee compete in this fashion. It is in this effect that the caffeine participates in the addictive process. Once a substance establishes its relationship with the receptors in the brain, the body then prefers to refill the receptors with that substance when needed, rather than use the natural brain chemicals.

In caffeinated soft drinks the phosphoric acid is another stimulant that depletes the alkaline mineral reserves, thus leaving the adrenals vulnerable to overstimulation. Withdrawal from caffeine often results in headaches and fatigue. But nutrition and herbs can help the transition to healthier beverages.

Many doctors consider caffeine to be the most detrimental drug available without a prescription. It is a strongly negative substance, and the body can take eighteen hours to reestablish a bio-positive energy after caffeine is introduced to the system. Caffeine is a strong central nervous system stimulator with strong addictive potential.

Caffeine also acts as a stimulus barrier in the brain to artificially help with depression, nervous exhaustion, and physical overwork. People with these conditions usually have a low level of norepinephrine—a natural stimulus barrier— available in the brain, a condition considered dangerous to health because it represents a diminished immune response.

Caffeine gives temporary support, both physiologically and psychologically. But along with that, caffeine introduces poisons known to increase catecholamines in the blood and alter blood sugar levels. Caffeine can produce heart palpitations, irregular heart beat, insomnia, high blood pressure, anxiety, ulcers, fibrocystic breast disease, birth defects, anxiety neurosis, and depression. All of these states can occur at levels as low as 250 milligrams per day. And one cup of strong coffee contains around 180 milligrams of caffeine.

In a 35-year study on coronary heart disease 1130 male medical students participated. Those who drank five cups of coffee or more per day were two to three times more at risk of getting clinical heart disease (myocardial infarction, angina, and cardiac arrest), as compared to non-coffee drinkers.

According to current FDA standards, caffeine should be classified as a dangerous drug. It would be made available for treatment of central nervous system depressant poisoning—but by prescription only! Yet caffeine is widely used. Billions of pounds of coffee are consumed each year. Caffeine is also found in pekoe tea, colas, and other soft drinks, as well as in headache remedies, like Anacin, Vanquish, and Excedrin. And, of course, chocolate also contains caffeine. This substance is so widely used that clinicians fail to consider it as a cause of, or contributor to, their patients' problems. It is estimated that 75% of the valium prescribed by doctors is for caffeine-related symptoms. And valium is terribly addictive!

The effects of caffeine vary greatly from person to person. Similarly, there is a variation of withdrawal symptoms, which usually begin with a headache, morning drowsiness, and irritability that lasts for two to four days. Many people find that tapering off is a less traumatic way to quit using caffeine. This is done by starting on Monday using decaf coffee in place of regular coffee several times a day, gradually abandoning the caffeine on Friday. After a weekend without coffee, the addiction is usually broken.

Natural therapies, in form of nerve support, adrenal support, basic nutritional support, and amino acid (neurotransmitter precursers) support can help minimize the withdrawal symptoms and help rebuild the natural function and energy of the body.

A curious fact is that most addictions alter a person's awareness of the problem. On our clinical questionnaire we ask how much caffeine is used. A person may respond: "Two cups a day." Then the spouse adds: "Well, that's before breakfast, but you also have coffee at the office and a coke when you come home."

Caffeine use often interferes with the action of natural therapies. It can inhibit the effectiveness of herbs and neutralize or antidote homeopathic remedies. Here is a clinical example. In 1987, a post-menopausal woman complained of debilitating fatigue. Evaluation via electropuncture indicated extreme adrenal fatigue. The woman's hair analysis showed burn-out. She refused to quit coffee but wanted to try a nutritional program. After two months of natural therapies, there was no significant improvement.

The woman's physician put her on a high dose of estrogen which helped her to feel better. After seven months on estrogen therapy, the woman developed lumps in her breasts. With her doctor's permission she consulted to see if any natural remedies would help her to reduce or delete the estrogen drug therapy. The woman had read that the herb Pfaffia (Suma) and the mineral Boron could function as estrogen substitutes in the body.

The client attempted this therapy along with some additional natural support, but without results. After three months of increasing fatigue and concomitant coffee use, she abondoned the natural therapies. Instead, she returned to a lower dose of estrogen, since the breast lumps had diminished.

A year later, the woman consulted to break her coffee habit. This we accomplished, but her deep fatigue returned. However, this time the natural therapies began to work. Four months later, and the client still free of the coffee habit, her adrenal glands showed improvement. Two months after this, we returned to the exact program used in 1987, when she first consulted. This time the program obtained effective results. Today, the client remains on a medium health maintenance program. She has good energy, does not take any medications, and does not show any further osteoporotic bone density loss.

In the case of this client it was her coffee drinking which increased her fatigue. The coffee habit also contributed to the breast problems. Most importantly, the coffee rendered herbs and homeopathic remedies ineffective. By breaking the coffee addiction, the client opened up a whole new level of health along with the ability for natural remedies to work.

TEA. Hot tea and iced pekoe tea (black tea) also contain caffeine, as do herbal teas with yerba mate or guarana. The caffeine of these beverages does not jolt the system immediately as coffees do, because the caffeine molecule is more complex, and the body requires a little time to break it down.

Significantly, the ritual of tea and crumpets in the afternoon is more than just social. The crumpets, cookies, and jams provide a dose of sugar to "lift" a person's sagging blood sugar levels right away. The caffeine in tea, which is time-released, keeps the artificial stimulation going through the entire evening.

The tannic acid in tea can contribute to poor health by its ability to bind with iron and interfere with the assimilation of iron. Iron poor blood is synonymous with fatigue, and the need for the caffeines in tea for energy is reinforced.

The bottom line is simply this: i f a person requires tea to feel better, then something is lacking in the overall health picture. Energy should be stable and of long supply in a human being. Herbal teas do not contain caffeine and tannic acids and can offer all the comfort, delightful taste, and ritual of tea without the overstimulation of the body or nutritional interference that black tea causes. Many delightful herbal tea blends are available these days.

CAFFEINATED SODAS. In the old days, when soft drinks were invented back in the 1930s, colas used to contain cocaine. The name Coke or Coca Cola referred to the coca or cocaine drug in the product. When coca was prohibited by law, the caffeine from the kola nut remained in the drink to addict the consumers. Without the cocaine in the beverage, the kola as well as the sugar contents were strengthened.

The financial success of the coca cola product was, and still is, based on its ability to addict the consumer to it, thereby ensuring continued sales.

As other sodas entered the market place, their success was based also on their ability to provide caffeine and sugar to addict the public. Even non-cola drinks had caffeine added for this reason. Names like Dr. Pepper attest to the purpose of the beverage—to artificially pep up the person drinking it.

One soft drink, marketed around 1987 and boasting the name Jolt, was advertised with the slogan: "Twice the sugar, twice the caffeine." At least the manufacturer was honest and did not try to hide the drink's addictive qualities behind such slogans as "new generation," or "the real thing," or behind endorsements by sports celebrities and popular movie idols.

Although this section is focused on caffeine in sodas, we should mention that the phosphoric acid in sodas removes the calcium from the body, causing the body to deplete calcium from its own bones to maintain health. When the blood becomes too acidic (a condition which can cause death), the body mobilizes calcium to buffer the acid to maintain the proper pH (acid/alkaline balance) in the blood. The richest supply of calcium in the body is in the bones from which the body borrows it whenever necessary. The calcium that buffers the phosphoric acid is excreted in the urine and lost from the body. For this reason sodas are directly related to the crippling bone disease osteoporosis.

Fortunately, today there are viable and delicious alternatives to addictive beverages. There are fragrant herb teas to replace caffeine-based coffees and teas. There are fruit juice and spring water sodas, such as Sundance sodas. These do not contain high fructose corn sweetener, and stand on their own as delicious and refreshing soft drinks. They still have a fruit sugar content and carbonization, but are a major improvement over the other sodas available.

In the '60s and '70s, if people chose not to drink addictive beverages, they simply did without them. But today, such a commitment to health is much easier since the substitutes for addictive drinks are readily available, tasty, reasonably priced, and not the least bit second-rate.

Researchers have set 200 mg of caffeine per day as the danger zone above which a person may experience detrimental symptoms and damage to the nervous system. Here are some tables to help you figure an accurate estimate of daily caffeine intake.

Source	Mg	x	Servings	=	Mg
Cappuccino	186	x	_____	=	_____
Espresso	192	x	_____	=	_____
Dripolated coffee	146	x	_____	=	_____
Percolated coffee	110	x	_____	=	_____
Instant coffee	72	x	_____	=	_____
Tea bag (5 min. steep)	47	x	_____	=	_____
Tea bag (1 min. steep)	29	x	_____	=	_____
Loose tea (5 min. steep)	40	x	_____	=	_____
Hot chocolate	5	x	_____	=	_____
Kahlua (per ounce)	44	x	_____	=	_____
Coke, classic	65	x	_____	=	_____
Dr. Pepper	61	x	_____	=	_____
Dr. Pepper, diet	54	x	_____	=	_____
Mountain Dew	56	x	_____	=	_____
Tab	49	x	_____	=	_____
Pepsi	43	x	_____	=	_____
R.C. Cola, diet	33	x	_____	=	_____
Diet Rite Cola	32	x	_____	=	_____
Chocolate candy bar	24	x	_____	=	_____
Anacin (per tablet)	32	x	_____	=	_____
Aqua-ban (per tablet)	00	x	_____	=	_____
Bivarin (per tablet)	200	x	_____	=	_____
Caffedrine (per tablet)	200	x	_____	=	_____
Dristan (per tablet)	16	x	_____	=	_____
Empirin (per tablet)	32	x	_____	=	_____
Excedrin (per tablet)	64	x	_____	=	_____
Midol (per tablet)	32	x	_____	=	_____
No-doz (per tablet)	100	x	_____	=	_____
Pre-mens Forte (per tab.)	100	x	_____	=	_____
Vanquish (per tablet)	33	x	_____	=	_____
OTHER	_____	x	_____	=	_____

TOTAL CAFFEINE PER DAY = _____

Deleting caffeine from your life can help you feel much better. After quitting, people are amazed how much their attitude improves and their enjoyment of life increases. One

patient reports: "Prior to quitting coffee, I could not have believed what an improvement its avoidance would make! I'm
still in the rat race, but now I'm in control. My PMS symptoms just vanished, my energy is even, not frenetic, and I'm
basically much happier."

Another note in our files contains the remark: "I stopped
drinking coffee, followed the Systemic Program, and avoided
a mastectomy!" It should be well heeded that caffeine is a
major contributor to fibrocystic disease, both breast and uter-
ine types.

**"That settles it, Carl! . . . From now on,
you're getting only decaffeinated coffee!"**

Few people realize that the body is inherently designed to have great energy on its own, without stimulants. A return to natural health brings back the natural energy. This natural energy is characterized by a calm, enduring, and vital well-being.

CHOCOLATE

Chocolate is discussed in a category by itself, because it is a serious addiction for some people. For others, it can be of little concern. Along with its sugar and caffeine content, chocolate is high in the minerals copper and magnesium, which are involved in the biochemical processes of human energy. People with low, or high, copper levels can crave chocolate; with low levels, because copper is needed; with high levels, because the copper is locked in the tissues and not available to the body. Magnesium is required for enzyme and neurotransmitter functions. Chocolate only provides a short-term lift, followed by low energy, mood changes, and often depression. And like the nicotine in tobacco, the alkaloids in chocolate can function as a stimulus barrier in the brain, providing a sense of solace, and a feeling-response similar to being loved. Some therapists say: "A hug a day keeps the chocolate away!"

Chocolate is a highly ALLERGENIC substance. Many people's chocolate cravings are not primarily for caffeine or sugar. Instead, these cravings are what is known as an allergy-addiction syndrome. This means that people crave things to which they are allergic. Inevitably, the alcoholic is allergic to grain or yeast, the coffee drinker to the coffee bean. Tobacco is a universal allergen, and everyone is sensitive to it to some degree. Some people are allergic to chocolate.

Chocolate addiction often begins in childhood. The parents, or grandparents, give the child some chocolate. The ensuing allergy symptoms may or may not be noticed, such as a little hyperactivity, irritability, runny nose. The next day the child is cranky, but improves after "earning" a candy bar. Parents quickly recognize that a Hershey's Kiss calms the irritable child. Therefore, candy is used as a behavior modification tool. And thus occurs the beginning of a detrimental

85

addiction and the start of future allergies, such as asthma, hives, poison ivy sensitivity, hypoglycemia, and so forth.

The chocolate, however, is rarely suspected because it provides such a seemingly positive effect. People need to be educated that when a food item is a quick "pick-me-up" or a helper, there is an allergy or sensitivity present.

People crave what they are allergic to because the body adapts to it and becomes dependent. In essence, the body teaches itself that the poisonous substance is non-toxic. The body becomes accustomed to adapting so that dependency is established, and it wants to avoid withdrawal symptoms.

A patient commented that once she ate a single piece of chocolate she "felt hungrier than ever," and that "one piece led to another." This is a typical food allergy symptom, that the craving is difficult to satisfy. Such an allergy can hit people with the force of a cyclone—an apparently absolute need to eat the substance.

A common side effect of chocolate addiction is obesity, particularly from water retention. The body's response to the chocolate allergen/toxin is to pad it with water to minimize its effect. Once the allergen is eliminated from the diet, dramatic weight (water) loss can occur.

One patient reports: "I lost 11 pounds of water weight in 11 days after quitting chocolate and following the Systemic Program. In the following eighteen weeks on the program I lost 42 pounds, of which 30 were obviously fat." A comment is needed here: this person was not on a weight-loss program. The weight loss happened automatically, because the person was on a program designed for good health.

Chocolate addiction affects the limbic part of the brain, which is the control center responsible for emotions, memory, sleep, appetite, sexuality, and blood pressure. Accompanying disorders in those areas are common with chocolate addiction. Clinically, we have found that a trio of herbal formulas performs exceptionally well together to stabilize imbalances in this area—B (Brain), Gb (Pituitary), and I (Eye). The program is used one week on, one week off, for four cycles. The manufacturer of these supplements is now putting all three together in one package under the name Smart Pak. These formulas have proven themselves to help people in transition from chocolate reliance to a more optimal level of health.

There is another reason why chocolate can be habit forming. It increases the natural opioid brain chemical, enkephalin, a narcotic brain chemical that can be as addictive as heroin. This means that chocolate causes a reserve, or emergency-only, system to become activated when it is not really needed. This can create an imbalance in the number of filled enkephalin receptor sites and give the body a false feeling of well being—a condition which cannot be maintained without the reapplication of chocolate.

While on the subject of chocolate and allergy-addictions, we should mention that wheat, dairy products (cow cheese, milk), and commercial eggs are major food allergens. Commercial cage eggs are known offenders, because they are frequently exposed to pesticides, but yard eggs usually are not. Corn, coffee, white potatoes, and often rice are also major food allergens. Because such potentially dangerous, common foods are so readily available, many people follow a dietary concept, called the Four Day Rotation Diet. Basically, they rotate foods so that they do not eat the same food twice in a four-day period.

Food rotation is beneficial for most people. It encourages a greater variety of foods, maximizes nutritional intake, and minimizes flaws in dietary selections. It also relieves the immune system of unnecessary responses, thus saving energy.

Dr. Robert Atkins, M.D., author of several diet books, writes regarding excessive weight: "If you have such a disorder, you don't need to eat less, you need to eat differently. It's also important to stay away from any foods to which you've developed an intolerance. How do you know which ones these are? Well, you may notice that occasionally, after you eat a certain food, you fall asleep, get extremely irritable, or feel ravenous. If you have a metabolic disorder, or intolerances, certain foods can be truly addicting. Chocolate is the quintessential example. This kind of addiction is indistinguishable from the alcoholic's addiction to drinking—and, like it, cannot be managed by moderation, only by abstinence."

If such attention to diet seems odd or unnatural, remember that the alarming increase in the numbers of allergic people and the devastating effects of allergies are often a result of environmental pollutants, such as industrial chemicals, gas fumes, and agricultural pesticides, for example. These pollutants, when combined with a stressful pace of life, weaken the immune system, and finally the system can no longer cope with such stressful conditions.

People with chocolate cravings can work nutritionally to break the allergic-addictive reaction, build the immune system, and stabilize their body chemistry so that a higher degree of health is realized. Chocolate craving is a specific symptom which points to an altered manifestation of the addicted person's life force, the bioenergy. Understanding this situation leads to the correct remedy, correct transition program, and correct nutritional maintenance.

EXCESSIVE SALT

Salt has been much maligned—and to some extent unjustly—in recent years. Therefore, the key in this discussion is EXCESSIVE use of salt. Virtually every chemical reaction in the body takes place in a salt water medium. Sugar is burned in a salt solution. Nerves transmit in a salt solution. For these reasons, salt is important to health.

Salt, from the earth or sea, is important in maintaining proper osmotic pressure in the body. But an excessive amount becomes a toxin and contributes to high blood pressure as well as stimulation of the adrenals to work more than they should. The organic salts from vegetables do not perform the osmotic function as well as earth or sea salt, since they are more easily broken down to sodium plus chloride, used as pH buffers, and chemical reactions which maintain life.

There is a fundamental difference in the molecular bonding of organic (covalent) and inorganic (ionic) salts. But both types of salt are required for health, though undoubtedly the organic salts are the most important.

Inorganic salt, such as table salt, supports the body's electrical system, whereas the inner cell uses only the organic or plant-derived salts. This means that there is some value in a little whole, natural salt. But there is harm in using too much, particularly when salt becomes a stimulant and is used in a quantity that the body needs to eliminate. People with very salty perspiration are probably eating too much table salt and should rely on vegetables more.

The best source of organic salt (sodium chloride) for cellular energy is green leafy vegetables, okra, and raw goats' milk. Many people have too much inorganic salt in their diets and not enough organic salt from vegetables. People with proper amounts of vegetables, about 75% of their diet, require very little earth or sea salt, but there is still a small requirement.

A lack of sodium in the body contributes to arthritis, ulcers, and a host of acidosis-based diseases. Sodium is a soft mineral whereas calcium is a hard mineral. Sodium provides elasticity and flexibility to tissues. It is essential to the stomach because it helps protect the stomach tissue from the harsh hydrochloric acid.

And, when too many acid foods and substances are used, such as sodas, red meat, and processed foods, the sodium reserves are called upon along with calcium to neutralize them and to help maintain proper blood pH.

The joints are normally rich in sodium. But if it becomes depleted, the calcium left behind causes hardness or arthritic symptoms. Table salt cannot replace this sodium, because the organic sodium is required. An excellent way to replenish sodium in the body is through vegetable juices and homemade soups.

Many addictive activities cause an acid pH. Thus addictions lead to arthritis, rheumatism, neuritis, and neuralgia. Many nutritionists recommend a glass of carrot and celery juice daily for arthritic clients. People with arthritic tendencies often notice great improvement when they return to the fundamentals of health: good diet, strong digestion, proper assimilation, and effective elimination. These are the areas in which your natural health counselor is best suited to help.

Salt free diets can be harmful! Salt is needed to make blood and to insure proper kidney function. Salt keeps the spark in the battery, so to speak. Some people get dizzy when they get out of a warm bath or hot tub. This can be due to a temporary lack of salt which was sweated out.

Some researchers advocate taking a salt water bath—two pounds of sea salt to a tub of water—to replenish electrolytes. Salt free diets lead to poor quality blood. Such a diet may appear to be beneficial for a person with thick blood or hypertension, but poor quality blood causes fatigue, lethargy, and exhaustion.

The use of table salt should be minimized, because it is subjected to extreme temperatures in processing. Many other mineral factors are depleted in table salt, and anti-caking agents are added to it. A natural, unprocessed sea salt would be a good choice, if such can be found. The label specifying "sea salt" is no guarantee that the salt has not been heated to 400 degrees Fahrenheit, the trace minerals removed, and anti-caking agents added. The label just means that the salt originally came from the sea. But if you think about it, all salt comes from the sea, even if it was mined inland. The real issue is how salt is processed. There are companies that provide real salt, unprocessed, with trace minerals intact, to the market. These salts can be verified because they will cake.

Some people add sea water to their distilled water to enliven it and give it some substance. Usually one teaspoon per gallon is used. This does not make the water salty or fishy tasting. By adding sea water to their drinking water, people avoid the salt shaker, maintain a good quality blood, and add a little spark to their soft drinking waters, such as distilled or reverse osmosis water. Bottled, purified sea water is inexpensive and available at health food stores.

Distilled water needs this treatment with sea water to make it biologically active. Because this water contains a heat-altered molecule it is not biologically compatible with the body (as seen by the rise in leukocytes in the blood) until the body alters it. In the book, *Pro-Vita! Diet*, (Tips, 1989) the water treatment is discussed in more detail. Distilled water is a good cleansing water, but not optimal for health. But when a teaspoon of sea water per gallon is added and the water sits in the sun for a few hours, then the distilled water becomes biologically compatible and does not cause a rise in leukocytes.

Again, the message here is balanced use of salt. There are so many opinions and arguments concerning salt. But when people understand the law of life known as balance, they also understand that organic vegetable salts are the foundation of health, with a pinch of natural salt for spark.

7

SOCIALLY ACCEPTED ADDICTIONS

In this chapter we discuss addictive substances which are socially acceptable in contrast to hard drugs which are not. Although the use of marijuana is not legal, we are including this substance here because it is so frequently associated with other accepted addictive activities. Also, we are listing tobacco and marijuana together here because they are both plant substances which are most commonly introduced to the body via the respiratory system, that is, people smoke them. And, the disruptions of these two substances to the body are bioenergetically similar, although each causes different damage as well.

TOBACCO

We will start with a brief focus on tobacco. The chapter, entitled "How to Stop Smoking," will provide more in-depth information on tobacco and its effects on the human body and spirit.

In addition to hundreds of potentially dangerous chemicals, tobacco contains several stimulatory chemicals, including cadmium (a toxic metal much more harmful than nicotine), nickel carbonyl (antagonist to the healing mineral zinc), benzol-a-pyreme (a carcinogen), and nicotine (an insecticide). Nicotine performs a dual role: it stimulates the adrenals and also blocks nerve impulses to the brain. Tobacco users find both pseudo energy and solace in their drug.

But even the federal government, which for years subsidized the tobacco industry, now admits that smoking tobacco causes 360,000 deaths a year, as reported by the U.S. Public Health Service in 1988. Lung cancer is among the leading causes of death in the United States. And a recent federal health report stated that deaths from lung cancer increased among women by 44 percent from 1979 to 1986. In fact, lung cancer has surpassed breast cancer as the most common cause of cancer death among women in the United States.

Tobacco affects the body by directly stimulating the adrenals and pushing them to exhaustion, causing thereby the need for constant re-stimulation. Marijuana, with its high cadmium content, moves quickly through the hypoglycemic (low blood sugar) cycle, thus exhausting the adrenals, thyroid, pancreas, and liver.

Bioenergetically, tobacco use inhibits the cell's ability to accept nutrients and release metabolic waste products. Smoking effects the permeability of the cell membrane, thickens arteries, limits the flow of blood, and becomes a cause of impotence when the penis arteries are affected.

Health Edco of Waco, Texas, was kind enough to provide the following information on tobacco use, cigarettes, pipe, cigars, and smokeless tobacco. This information is included here as a reminder that tobacco use is very detrimental to health. We thank Health Edco for the permission to use the information in this book.

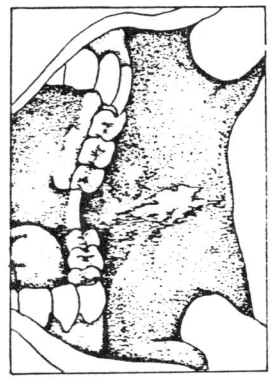

LEUKOPLAKIA
is a wrinkled, white leathery patch which often resembles the hide of an elephant. Leukoplakia is a precancerous condition caused by irritation from direct contact with dangerous ingredients contained in tobacco juice. Approximately one in every 20 cases of leukoplakia becomes cancerous.

CANCER OF THE ESOPHAGUS
is also associated with the use of smokeless tobacco. This cancer causes difficulty in swallowing and a sensation of blockage behind the sternum.

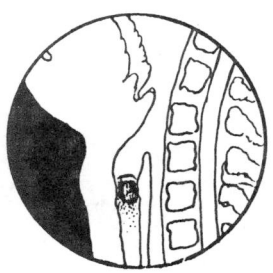

CANCER OF THE LARYNX (VOICE BOX)

occurs more commonly in men than in women, most often after the age of 40. Following surgical removal of the diseased larynx, patients are fitted with an electronic voice box.

CANCER OF THE CHEEK

is the most common form of oral cancer. The white, ulcerated, round area represents cancer caused by chronic irritation

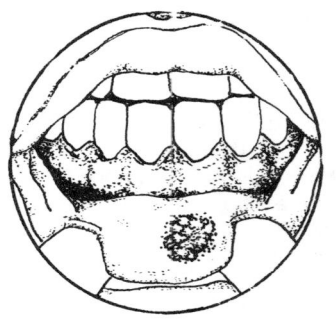

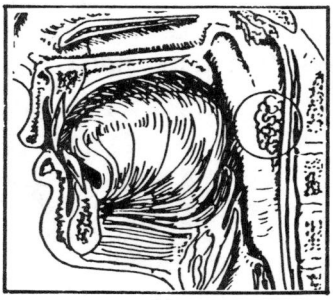

CANCER OF THE PHARYNX

occurs more commonly in smokeless tobacco users than nonusers because there is a tendency to swallow some of the tobacco juice.

CANCER INSIDE THE LIP

is another common occurrence in smokeless tobacco users. That's because the snuff is held for long periods of time between the teeth and lip.

BROWN STAINED TEETH

caused by residue from the mixture of saliva and tobacco, which forms tobacco juice.

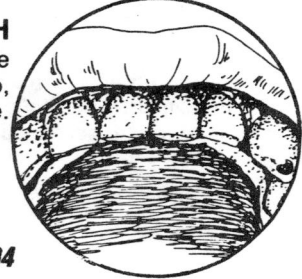

BLACK HAIRY TONGUE

is a particularly gross condition and while it is not cancerous it is both ugly and devastating from a social standpoint. The stain, which resembles small, black hairs, is caused by a combination of food, tobacco and germs.

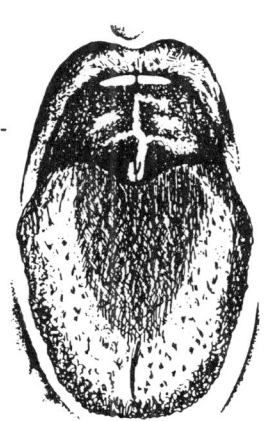

HEART ATTACKS

When smokeless tobacco is taken into the body the oxygen-carrying capacity of the blood is *decreased,* while the clotting rate is *increased.* Hypertension, combined with arteriosclerosis, can cause a fatal heart attack. Heart attacks are the number one killer of Americans.

CANCER OF THE URINARY BLADDER

Smokeless tobacco users have a higher incidence of bladder cancer because chemicals from nicotine are absorbed into the bloodstream and excreted through the urine. These carcinogens are continously in contact with the lining of the bladder.

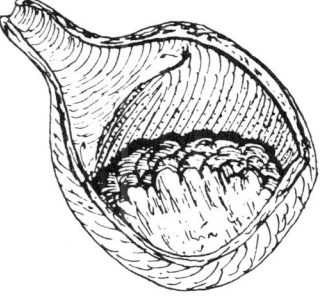

95

STOMACH ULCERS

are also more common in smokeless tobacco users than nonusers. That's because some of the hazardous ingredients found in tobacco juice are swallowed. Stomach ulcers may hemorrhage, perforate or obstruct the passage of food.

ARTERIOSCLEROSIS

is the medical term for hardening of the arteries. Deposits of irregularly distributed yellow patches of fat and minerals form on the inside of the arteries. Arteriosclerosis is the basic condition responsible for most heart attacks, strokes, high blood pressure and senility.

MARIJUANA

Both tobacco and marijuana cause the body to adapt to their toxins and effects. Marijuana is considered by many people to be non-physiologically addictive. However, this is simply not the case. In effect, marijuana is both physiologically and psychologically addictive, although much less profoundly so than hard drugs, such as heroin. Phelps and Nourse, in their book, *The Hidden Addiction* (1986), describe marijuana as a very addictive drug. Above all, in their opinion, marijuana is a subtle drug which insidiously alters perceptions of space and time.

Residues from tobacco and marijuana can remain in the body for years, especially in the lower liver lobe, causing a bioenergetic disruption. In working with electro-acupuncture equipment, it is fascinating to test the homeopathic remedy cannabis sativa (which is potentized marijuana) on the liver meridian. It commonly tests positive on people who remark: "But I haven't used marijuana in fifteen years!"

But even after many years of non-use the residue is still present and registers a disruptive bioenergetic pattern. From the bioenergetic perspective we find that marijuana, used in a recreational context, is detrimental to the bioenergetic field of the human being.

Marijuana in Northern California has been bred to be the most powerful in the world. Advanced botanical propagation and techniques have produced a 200% increase in the active ingredient, tetrahydrocannabinol, resulting in greater addictive properties. It is a new drug in its stronger potency. It definitely causes a dependency, particularly with people who have a tendency to melancholy or lack a constructive outlet for their frustrations and dissatisfactions.

Heavy marijuana users often have a very healthy disdain of the government, bureaurocracies, the futility of war, and the absurdities of society. But instead of being able to channel their perspective into positive changes, they end up being apathetic and unproductive. Their passive attitudes of "Hey, man, just leave me alone; I won't bother you, and you don't bother me; I'm not hurting anyone," cripple their ability to create a dynamic life or a positive society, because they quickly become the effect of the system they disdain. Marijuana is for losers. It helps them find solace in dropping out and thus making a weak, ineffective statement about their disapproval of the way the world has gone.

It is well documented that marijuana alters a person's outlook by interfering with certain brain centers, thus manifesting apathy, unproductivity, mañana-complexes (let's do it tomorrow), and a mellowness which users call "peace" with nature, but which actually resembles a state similar to "jellyfishness". The only time when heavy marijuana users really get riled up is when someone threatens their supply or intent to use marijuana.

It seems appropriate here to write a few words on the metaphysical aspects of the trap of marijuana on the human spirit. If you are of a scientific orientation and do not give credence to as-of-yet undocumented orientations, then this information will seem a little off-beat. But to the millions of people who are aware, or are becoming aware, of their bioenergetic potentials, we want to provide this knowledge. This information originates from my clinical work with Jamaican musicians whose Rastafarian religion requires the use of marijuana.

Marijuana disrupts the auric (bioenergetic) field of the body by literally perforating it with tiny holes. These holes are virtually a sieve to the healthy energies of the body, allowing them to leak out or dissipate. This is the bioenergetic side of the issue why heavy marijuana users are such dissipated people. A leak exists in their bioenergy system and therefore they just never get a full charge out of life.

These tiny auric holes often resemble a shotgun blast. Thousands of tiny, black holes have dotted through what previously was a bright auric field. Not only do these holes allow vital energies to dissipate out of the person, they allow negative influences to enter the human field. These negative influences can be as mild as outside energetic waves which make a person prone to bacterial and viral infections, or as severe as psychic entity attachment whereby the person flirts with entity-possession.

In such a case, a disembodied entity can attach itself to the person's field at a prominent hole, usually close to the naval, and feed off the person's life energies very similar to a vampire. It can stay attached or it can come and go. Entities such as these are usually seeking drug gratification through a physical vehicle, something normally denied them. The entity itself is an unfulfilled "addict," and the hapless victim is the substance. The victim becomes susceptible, because the drug (marijuana, alcohol, cocaine, speed, heroin, and occasionally tobacco) can cause a bioenergetic lesion, a prominent hole, which invites the entity in. Some people have enough personal energy to repair the damage of drug use and avoid such frightening experiences, others do not.

The human auric field also serves as a protective, egg-shaped bubble which keeps the human experience intact in its own world, and keeps lower influences out of it. Marijuana disrupts that field, leaving the user susceptible to lower influences if the body cannot patch up the damage daily.

In clinical work, particularly with kinesiology, it is easy to determine when a person is a chronic marijuana user. When the remedies are introduced to the person's field by placing them on the person's abdomen, parotid gland, or in their hand, they will test well, but will not hold to the overstress test. The overstress test demonstrates if the substance has enough power to initiate a healing response. Remedies and healing herbs will look good initially, but will not effect a complete repair. Once again, the person is like a sieve, and the positive or sustaining energy leaks out before the body can respond with full healing potential. These people need to keep repeating the remedies and keep taking the herbs in an attempt to get more energy in than leaks out, so to speak.

I first noticed this phenomenon while working with the group of Jamaican musicians of the Rastafarian religious sect. Since their religion, indigenous to Jamaica, advocates the daily use of ganja, or marijuana, they are chronic users. The remedies and nutritional formulas would help at first, but never carry them to the next plateau of health. Yet, these people, who were attaining financial success through their music, wanted good health, but always had to be on a therapeutic program just to break even. We found that the Wheelwright bioextract formula, Tai Ra Chi, helped to seal the leaks energetically so that herbs and nutrition could work better. But the clients constantly undermined the success of the program with marijuana. Although I no longer see these individuals clinically, they still order the Tai Ra Chi formula because it helps them function better—"good for the attitude, you know, mon".

Probably the most important detrimental effect of marijuana use is that it impairs the immune system. Marijuana smoke contains even more carcinogenic substances than tobacco smoke. In the *Harvard Medical School Letter*, Vol. 4, No. 5, it was reported that marijuana use was linked to cancer and AIDS, since it diminishes the immune response.

Since many people who used marijuana in the sixties and seventies were misinformed about the side effects of marijuana, it bears mention here that marijuana damages the brain, damages the lungs, impairs brain function, interferes with the thinking, learning, and memory processes, and harms the reproductive organs. Marijuana affects the limbic area of the brain and contributes to feelings of apathy, paranoia, alienation, and insecurity. Such attitudes greatly affect a person's ability to be successful and enjoy life.

Since marijuana can affect the unborn child, mothers must never smoke or be in the environment of marijuana during pregnancy. Men who smoke prior to fathering a baby can be passing on weakened genetic information.

A CASE HISTORY: Clinically, I consulted with a four-year-old girl for chronic ear and throat infections, frequent upper respiratory tract infections, and hyperactivity. She had many signs which pointed to the homeopathic remedy Tuberculinum, including weight loss, slow physical development, and fear of dogs, but that remedy brought no results. Herbal therapies were effective in helping the acute problems, but the problems would reoccur.

The mother confided that the father was a chronic user of marijuana for twenty years. During a conversation with the father, he stated: "You can't tell me that marijuana interferes with sex and makes you impotent. I fathered a child after sixteen years of daily marijuana use."

I did not comment on my suspicion that perhaps the preconceptual marijuana use was responsible for the child's poor health.

The mother had used many homeopathic remedies on the child without clear guidance. She had already administered many of the "clearing" remedies in a variety of potencies, including Nux Vomica, Sulphur, Thuja, and Silicea for whatever reason she had at the time. Based on this indiscriminate mixture of previous remedies, I gave the child the remedy Cannabis Sativa 200C and followed it two weeks later with Tuberculinum 10M with immediate results.

To me, this situation means that the marijuana use by the father was, in effect, a miasm inhibiting the child's health and inhibiting the effectiveness of the appropriate remedy until it was "cleared". Six months later, after two bouts of ear aches which did not have to be treated, and one bout of respiratory coughing and heavy mucous expectoration which was treated acutely, the child simply blossomed and came into her own. After three years now, no further sign of the above mentioned symptoms is evident.

Delta-9-tetrahydrocannabinol (THC), the active ingredient in marijuana, stays in the blood stream for about six days after partaking. But its residues can stay in the liver for years, undetectable except by electro-acupuncture equipment or biopsy. Many people have learned to beat the urine-based drug tests by taking the herb goldenseal and vitamin C. But they are not beating the impartial laws of bioenergetics, because goldenseal alone will not restore the proper human wave form and end the warp caused by auric lesions due to marijuana use. In his research for an effective herbal antibiotic, Wheelwright discovered that using goldenseal as a base ingredient, a high-oscillatory, herbal formula could be constructed to help people break a habit with an addictive substance. He called his formula GOLD which has become the predominant herbal antibiotic in natural medicine. Some herbalists apply it for any habit-breaking program with good success.

Although smoking marijuana is disruptive to the holistic health of the individual, it is a medicinal herb in the grand scheme of things. Marijuana is primarily an anti-nausea herb. In some instances, it can function as a pain reliever in the case of headaches. It is used illegally by some medical doctors in the U.S., and legally by many doctors in European nations, to offset the nausea of chemotherapy, so there is clinical data proving it to be an anti-nausea drug. On a more positive note, homeopathy offers anti-nausea remedies which do not have any detrimental side effects to the user.

It is fascinating how nausea is a healthy reaction of the body to the severe, systemic poisons used in chemotherapy, and how the drug, marijuana, can help overcome that side effect by quelling the chemically disturbed brain center. It is often the case in drug-medicine that one damaging drug is needed to offset the side effects of another damaging drug.

Research at the U.S. National Institute of Mental Health has isolated the gene which allows a person to get high from marijuana. Scientists are directing this research toward isolating the receptors in the brain that have medicinal applications for using marijuana-based medicines for blocking pain, relieving nausea, and sedative effects without impacting psychoactive receptors in an individual.

Some marijuana proponents claim that marijuana expands their consciousness. This may be true for some people if the absent-minded, slow motion fixation to the minute details of being stoned is a step to higher consciousness. I guess it is all relative where a person's consciousness starts out, because there is always a step higher. The problem with marijuana is that it bottoms out or tops out (however you want to look at it) at a low level and inflicts damage on the person's well-being in the process. Even if it is a step for a few individuals, somehow, toward greater awareness; a person cannot stay in kindergarten for ever! For these people, marijuana must drop away before any real progress can be realized. And once a person depends upon something external, that person is limited by the scope of that activity. The fact is, marijuana just is not taking people anywhere significant.

The war against marijuana will not be won by the government's C.A.M.P. (Citizens Against Marijuana Producers) agents cutting down plants, and it will not be won by TV personalities just saying "no". The war must be won in the human spirit by affirming life without the enslavement of addictive activities.

Life in this world perpetually deals us circumstances which can delay or withhold our true development into what we can be. This is the testing ground for spirit, and we must rise above the petty entrapments to our magnificent destiny. Making the break from the ubiquitous weeds (tobacco, marijuana, coca, poppy, kava kava, jimson weed, and so forth) which cripple us when we misuse them, is the doorway to new and exciting spiritual adventures.

TWO IRONIC STORIES. Life is fascinating. Here are two examples of how topsy-turvy the human condition is.

The first story relates to the absurdity that the U.S. government launches a campaign under the auspices of the Surgeon General to stop smoking, while concurrently subsidizing the tobacco industry financially to help the economy, and to keep tobacco farmers in business.

The June 2, 1988, edition of the *Austin American-Statesman* featured an article about the Texas Department of Mental Health and Mental Retardation's reluctance to comply with a U.S. government request to ban smoking in mental hospitals. T.D.M.H.M.R. stated that smoking "is a very substantial part of their [the patients'] life....If you restrict patients from smoking completely, tempers go up and they are agitated."

The article further quoted a T.D.M.H.M.R. spokesperson saying: "Smoking should be tolerated for therapeutic reasons." Evidently, the hospital employees give patients, or residents, cigarettes as incentives or behavior modification tools. The patient who is hooked on tobacco will comply, when needing a fix.

According to the article, T.D.M.H.M.R. also insisted that the patients have a right to smoke. On one hand, the state has decided that mental patients are incapable of caring for themselves in society, and thus are committed to hospital care. On the other hand, the officials claim that the institution should not interfere with the patients' right to poison their already imbalanced brains.

The interesting question is: how many residents of state hospitals and state schools are taught to smoke, so that the employees have an effective behavior modification tool?

This question becomes even more pervasive, when we consider the recent statements by U.S. Surgeon General C. Everett Koop. In his 618-page report on the nation's addictions, Koop described nicotine as addictive as cocaine and heroin. Consequently, he recommended strengthening the laws restricting the sale of tobacco products to minors, and to include requiring establishments, where tobacco is sold, to have a license.

But the real irony in this story is that the taxpayers pay for the cigarettes given out in the state hospitals! Each state hospital spends six to eight thousand dollars a year for behavior-mod cigarettes. Now such hospitals are buying big air purifiers to help clear the smoke. This story definitely fits into life's category "you can't win for losing."

The second story is also paradoxical. It has nothing to do with smoking directly. But since it is about pesticides and chemicals, it still relates to our topic under discussion.

Have you ever noticed how, in this world, truth is persecuted and lack of truth exalted? Well, the extent of the damage that pesticides and agricultural sprays cause to our health, rivers, and planet continues to be covered up. But the clinical nutritionists, using electro-acupuncture, Vega-test, Computron, Interro or radionics testing devices, are aware of the health-crippling effects of such toxic residues in people. These nutritionists often subscribe to research which originates from Germany, where bioenergetic practitioners are respected instead of being suppressed.

Why are such health hazards continued to be hushed-up? Because insecticides, pesticides, herbicides, and fungicides are big business ventures, backed up by companies with political clout. And they are a part of a big system — the agricultral system — which is run by the few and needed by all.

But when such financial or political clout is lacking, strange things happen. For example, a couple of years ago, the FDA stopped a fine manufacturer of homeopathic remedies from selling a remedy for insecticides. The FDA did not object to the company's twenty-five other remedies, but forbade the sale of the one called Insecticide Detox. This decision was not due to any particular ingredient in the homeopathic remedy, but because a remedy, called Insecticide Detox, implies that there is a reason to detoxify such chemicals from the body. Yet, European homeopathy produces remedies for Malathion; 2,4,D; 2,4,5,T, better known as agent orange; Dursban; Diazinon; Chlordane; DDT.; and Round-up among others. Americans are denied these remedies, because their existence admits an existing problem with toxic insecticides.

Now back to the story. One evening, the last two patients in the clinic were people who were improving their health by detoxifying themselves of chemical sprays—one for exposure to 2,4,5,T (agent orange) that occurred in New Zealand, the other for years of agricultural contact with malathion and Round-up. The devastating effects of these chemicals had significantly altered the clients' life-styles.

The agent orange victim had lost his hair. The farmer was prone to violent outbreaks involving both his family and strangers. Subsequently, both showed dramatic improvement from their nutritional work. Such improvement included that the hair grew back for the victim of agent orange, and the farmer's anti-social behaviors ceased.

While I was driving home that evening, a BMW passed me on the freeway, bearing a white bumper sticker with lovely blue letters that read:

PESTICIDES PROTECT
- people
- animals
- crops

And to think that if nutritionists make claims about a nutrient's ability to heal, they might spend time in jail!

It could be, however, that the defensive bumper sticker is a sign that people are beginning to catch on to the pesticide industry, and that the industry feels the need for rebuttal.

The manufacture and use toxic of pesticides must stop. It is a matter of survival for our planet. Such chemicals have been proven ineffective because the bugs adapt and mutate. And the chemicals poison us! And we don't adapt as fast as bugs! People interested in alternatives to pesticides can get valuable information from Gardens Alive (Natural Gardening Research Center), Hwy. 48, P.O. Box 149, Sunman, IN 47041.

Few people realize that chemical fertilizers and pesticides are addicting their lawns to the same dependency cycle that drug addicts experience. By depleting the soil and creating shallow roots which cannot extract normal nutrients from the deeper top soil, residential lawns become dependent on chemical drugs, much less healthy, and more susceptible to fungus and disease. Besides, the toxic chemicals being applied to lawns are poisonous to children and animals. And the chemicals run off into our creeks and rivers. Fortunately, there are safe, effective, and extremely viable alternatives available. Visit your natural garden center!

Pesticides are linked with addictive tendencies and accumulate in our bodies. The FDA approves a pesticide if an injection of it does not kill a rat; but in doing so the agency only determines acute poisoning.

Pesticides chronically weaken our immune and energy systems. Organophosphates, such as indoor fumigants, Dursban, Diazinon, Malathion, Orthene, etc., destroy the body's enzymes which are vital to effective nerve function. Exposure to these chemicals occurs through breathing, eating, drinking, and skin contact.

Organic farming provides fruits, vegetables, eggs, meats, and dairy products that are produced with ecologically sound methods and natural materials. Such organic produce builds the health of our soil and prevents synthetic contaminants from damaging our soil and water. You can support organic farming via the "Organic Foods Production Act of 1990," introduced by Senator Leahy as SB 2108. This act provides incentives to farmers to reduce the use of poisonous chemicals and use organic growing techniques instead.

ALCOHOL

Alcohol is a dangerous substance, affecting the body in many detrimental ways. But, at the same time, it produces pseudo energy. In fact, hard liquor is also known as liquid energy, because it acts so quickly. Have you ever wondered how alcoholics get around without eating? They are literally running on an alcohol energy system.

But hard liquor pushes and thereby stresses both the adrenal and thyroid glands before becoming a depressant. Alcohol stresses the pancreas and liver as well, causing a hypoglycemic cycle.

And, alcohol washes important zinc reserves out of the body. Recent findings on alcoholism, reported in the *Journal of Biosocial Research*, show that zinc deficiencies induce voluntary consumption of alcohol. Children of alcoholics were found to have reduced tissue levels of zinc, and thus have a higher risk of becoming alcoholics. Or, if alcoholism is avoided due to childhood trauma with alcoholic parents, an addiction to sugar is likely in such children.

The body's toxic reaction to alcohol is significant. Alcohol is converted to acetaldehyde in the liver, which then damages brain cells as well as liver cells, and generates numerous free radical oxidizers that can cause cancer. The body's important and rare trace mineral molybdenum is exhausted quickly by processing acetaldehyde. The effects of the processing of alcohol in the body are devastating, because the process is an enzymatically uncontrolled oxidation, or burning, of materials which releases destructive free radicals— molecules which damage tissue and cause cancer. Consequently, alcohol is a systemic poison.

Oxidizing alcohol is a high priority for the liver. In fact, the liver neglects many other duties, when alcohol is present, because it must work to break down alcohol at a rate of 1/2 ounce per hour. During the time when the liver is processing alcohol, other toxins accumulate, and nutritional functions are neglected. Therefore, alcohol robs the body of vital health.

Alcohol is an addictive drug, although not as universally addicting as heroin. Heroin is addictive to 99.9% of its users. Alcohol is selectively addictive to approximately 12% of its users. But susceptibility to alcohol addiction increases with years of use. Research on alcoholism reveals that the predisposing factor, making some people so easily addictive, is physiological and relates to heredity and biochemistry. For this reason alcoholism is classified as a disease. In effect, alcohol addiction is a physiological malfunction.

Hank Williams, Jr. sings: "Hangovers hurt more than they used to." If that becomes the case, a person needs to suspect a weakened liver and should begin the Liver Triad program to nutritionally support the most important organ in the body. For further information see the book, *The Liver Triad* (Tips, 1989).

Henry David Thoreau wrote in *Walden*: "It's never too late to give up your prejudices." In the past, people criticized alcoholics for their irresponsibility and lack of will power. But those people who were criticizing were not prone to alcohol addiction. To the alcoholic, the addiction is so compelling that he or she is virtually unable not to obey its command. The non-susceptible person finds it very difficult to understand this. To fully comprehend alcoholism and its myths, the book, *Under the Influence*, by Milam & Ketcham (1981) presents an excellent discourse.

For people who can tolerate alcohol use, because they do not have the predisposing imbalances, it is important to understand that, healthwise, the less alcohol, the better. More than just a small amount of alcohol will take a nutritional toll. Actually, alcohol occurs naturally in the human body. As alcohols are broken down, or oxidized, in the liver, a great deal of energy is released. But the body only needs a miniscule amount of alcohol.

To demonstrate the devastating health effects of alcohol consumption, Health Edco has generously supplied facts and drawings on the following pages.

Alcoholism is a disorder characterized by repeated drinking of alcoholic beverages to an extent that it interferes with the drinker's physical health, emotional health and social functioning. Most alcoholics are not derelicts, but are married, have a job and go to church. When taken as a group, the diseases associated with alcoholism constitute the third leading cause of disability and death in America.

VARICOSE VEINS OF THE ESOPHAGUS
Cirrhosis of the liver produces a secondary increase in blood pressure in the veins of the esophagus (food tube leading from the throat to the stomach). This pressure causes the veins to become stretched and dilated (varicose). Death from internal hemorrhaging may occur if these thin, ballooned-out veins rupture.

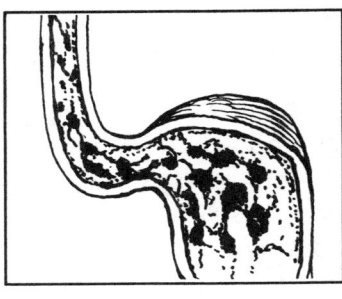

CANCER OF ESOPHAGUS
Due to an unknown chemical quality in alcoholic beverages, alcoholics have a far greater chance of developing cancer of the esophagus than do non-alcoholics. Cancer causes difficulty in swallowing and a sensation of blockage behind the sternum. Surgery is the only treatment, and the cure rate is very low.

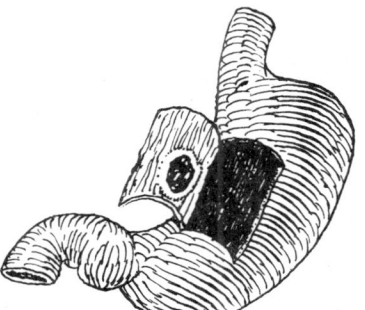

GASTRIC ULCERS

Alcohol is extremely irritating to the stomach and causes an over-secretion of stomach acids and enzymes. This increased acidity causes ulcers and prevents healing of existing ulcers. Stomach ulcers may hemorrhage, perforate, or obstruct passage of food. No ulcer patient should drink.

DUODENAL ULCERS

The duodenum is the first part of the small intestine which receives food from the stomach. Ulcers develop here for the same reason they develop in the stomach. Bleeding, obstruction, and perforation may be fatal complications of duodenal ulcers if patients continue to drink.

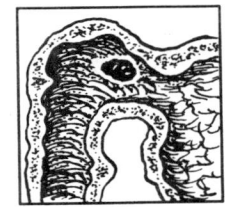

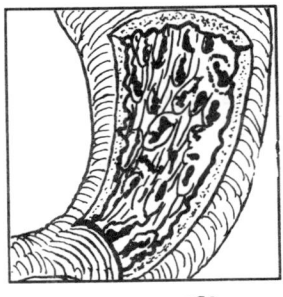

GASTRITIS

Heavy drinking is the most common cause of serious inflammation of the lining of the stomach. The mucosa becomes reddened with bleeding areas covered with thick, ropy mucus. Symptoms include nausea, vomiting, headache and pains in the stomach.

PANCREATITIS

The pancreas is a small organ lying in the uppermost portion of the abdomen, stretching from the duodenum on the right to the spleen on the left. It produces insulin and digestive enzymes vital to life. Inflammation of the pancreas is a serious illness characterized by severe abdominal pain, nausea and vomiting. Alcohol is directly poisonous to the pancreas, and 40% of pancreatitis patients are alcoholics.

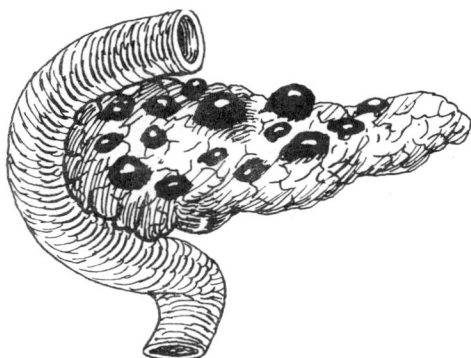

109

ALCOHOLIC HEPATITIS
This condition is characterized by fever, jaundice, swelling in the abdomen, and swelling of the feet. The liver is generally large, firm, tender and infiltrated with fat. Many patients die from this illness, some recover and others progress to develop cirrhosis.

FATTY LIVER
Excessive intake of alcohol can cause the liver to be infiltrated with droplets of fat. The liver becomes large and tense, and its color varies from yellow to green. When cut, the liver has doughy consistency, owing to the high fat content. Fatty liver may give few symptoms early in its course, but if drinking continues this abnormality will progress to cirrhosis and eventually to death.

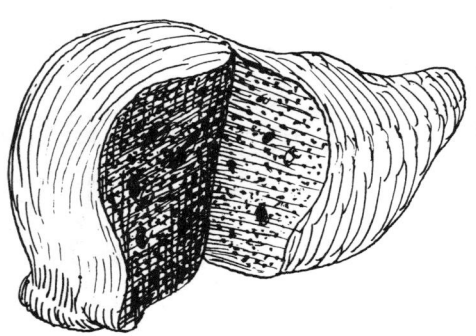

DEGENERATION OF THE CEREBELLUM
The cerebellum is the portion of the brain at the rear of the skull which controls equilibrium. Chronic alcoholics may develop a withering of the top portion of this organ with permanent loss of coordination.

NEURITIS
Prolonged intake of alcohol has a direct poisonous effect upon the nerves in the arms and legs. Symptoms include tingling, pins and needles sensations, burning, itching, numbness, weakness and paralysis. Treatment involves complete abstinence from alcohol, improved nutrition and vitamin supplementation.

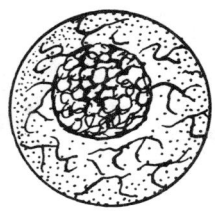

DELIRIUM TREMENS
Withdrawal from alcohol can cause physical and emotional suffering worse than withdrawal from heroin. The DT's begin with tremors, sweating and nausea. They progress to insomnia, profound confusion, delusions, hallucinations and convulsions. This serious complication may be fatal approximately 10% of the time.

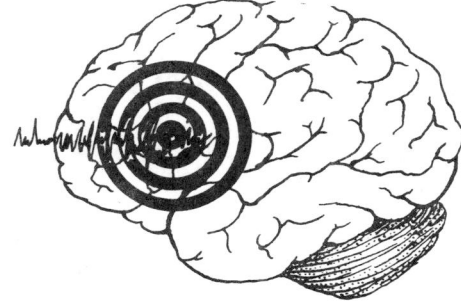

IMPOTENCY
Impotency refers to the inability of a man to sustain an erection satisfactory for normal sexual intercourse. Alcohol is one of the most common causes of impotency. The belief that alcohol is an aphrodisiac or sexual stimulant is pure nonsense. In acute alcoholism, the impotency may be caused by the depressant effect of the drug. In chronic alcoholism, impotency may be caused by neuritis, liver damage, malnutrition and other complications.

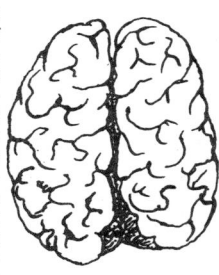

BIRTH DEFECTS
Many babies born of alcoholic women have abnormal development. They are underweight and their brain size is less than normal. The development of the heart may be incomplete and there may be a cleft palate. They continue to grow at a slower pace after birth and end up as smaller adults. Alcohol passes through the bloodstream of the mother into the uterus and placenta and directly into the unborn child. Pregnant women should avoid all drugs, including alcohol, particularly during the first three months of pregnancy.

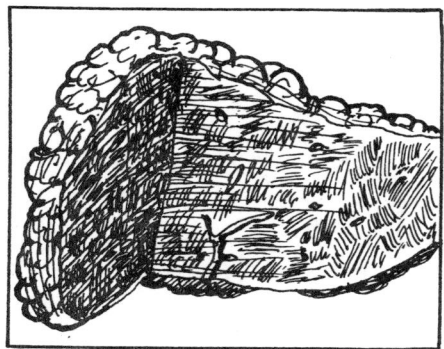

CIRRHOSIS
Cirrhosis is the seventh leading cause of death in America. Alcohol is the leading cause of cirrhosis. The cut surface of the liver may enlarge or shrink, depending on the stage of the disease. The outside surface is frequently rough and wrinkled like a prune. Symptoms include loss of weight, chronic nausea, vomiting, weakness, loss of sex drive, abdominal pains, bloating of the abdomen and hemorrhaging.

111

ACCIDENTS

Alcohol is a contributing factor in approximately 20% of all falls, 20% of accidental asphyxiations, 20% of drownings 20% of deaths from freezing, 25% of deaths attributed to choking on foods, 50% of all fire deaths, and well over 60% of all fatal automobile accidents.

CHILD ABUSE

Approximately 1 in every 100 American children are physically and psychologically severely abused at least once. Excessive drinking is a major factor in a large majority of these cases.

SUICIDE

Suicide is the tenth leading cause of death in America and the third leading cause of death below the age of 30. Alcohol is a factor in over 60% of all suicide attempts, successful and unsuccessful.

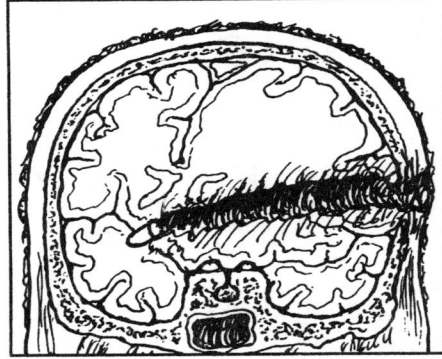

MURDER

Murder is the twelfth leading cause of death in America and the fourth leading cause of death below the age of 30. Alcohol is implicated in over 70% of all murders and other violent crimes.

WHY SOME PEOPLE DRINK MORE THAN OTHERS.

Do you know why some people can drink more alcohol than others? Why one drink makes some people tipsy while it takes four or five to loosen up others? The answer, to be found in the person's metabolic rate and nutrient levels, gives us insights into our individual biochemistry.

It is a stereotypic fact that men can drink more than women. This fact is undoubtedly responsible for the adage, "candy is dandy, but liquor is quicker," referring to how a man might improve his chances of an amorous encounter by uninhibiting a woman's better judgement via alcohol.

This apparent difference in alcohol consumption and its effects are discussed in the New England *Journal of Medicine* (January, 1990). The study examined why women were generally affected sooner by alcohol consumption. The research indicated that body weight was not the issue as generally assumed. Instead, the study pointed out that women absorbed 33% more alcohol through the stomach than men. This was due to a lower amount of the enzyme alcohol dehydrogenase in female stomachs. This enzyme detoxifies alcohol and therefore acts as a barrier when it is present in the stomach.

Alcohol dehydrogenase is dependent on the mineral zinc to function, and men generally have a higher level of zinc than women. In the stomach zinc slows the absorption rate of alcohol. High amounts of alcohol dehydrogenase are also found in the liver. This is why the liver is the primary alcohol detoxification organ. Any alcohol in the blood is transported to the liver for detoxification. Before it gets to the liver, it may pass through the brain and kill a few thousand cells, but eventually, the liver bears the burden of processing the alcohol out of the body. Some people find that after a bout of hepatitis or mononucleosis they lose the ability to process alcohol well, and that it affects them much more than before. During these liver diseases, the body sends copper to the liver to help fight the pathological organisms and secondary bacterial infections. Copper acts in opposition to zinc and thus the liver's ability to utilize zinc for the alcohol dehydrogenase's processes is diminished.

This is one biochemical example backing up the statement we often make to clients telling them that diseases of the liver "knock the stuffing out of the liver," and that a nutritional program is essential to regain better liver function. Full recovery usually does not happen by itself without specific nutritional support via the Liver Triad Program. Without such support, the weakened liver sets a lower homeostasis for the body, and the person's entire level of health operates on a lower level.

From an article in the *New York State Journal of Medicine*, (1950), we derive some insights on another reason why different people process alcohol at different rates. Dr. J. J. Smith proposes that adrenal (cortex) insufficiency sets the stage for alcohol addiction.

This is interesting from a nutritional or natural health perspective, because the adrenals are involved with a person's metabolic or oxidation rate. Fast oxidizers can process alcohol much better than slow oxidizers. For fast oxidizers, the enzyme reactions happen quicker and the alcohol is burned better. In the example of the fast oxidizer, because the alcohol helps maintain the rapid metabolic rate and high energy system, addiction is quite likely.

In the case of the slow oxidizer, or person with low adrenal function, the alcohol provides a boost to the lagging metabolic functions and temporarily relieves the depression states that are often associated with slow metabolic processes. Therefore the slow oxidizer has more than a passing interest in alcohol and can also fall prey to addiction.

The oxidation rates can be balanced with nutritional therapies. For this reason, supplementation with the Adrenal formula and the Nerve formula is a foundation for the Systemic program to help people break addictions. Additionally, proper nutritional support with other nutrients can help the body heal cirrhosis, fatty degeneration, and over-oxidation of the liver, and help correct abnormal iron values often associated with alcohol abuse.

ALCOHOL AND BRAIN CHEMISTRY. It is important to understand how ADDICTIONS AFFECT THE BRAIN. We are including the following information for your enlightenment and because knowledge represents power in overcoming addictions. The research was performed by Kenneth Blum, PhD, Chief, Division of Alcohol and Substance Abuse, University of Texas Health Science Center, San Antonio, Texas; and Michael C. Trachtenberg, PhD, Vice President, Research and Development, Matrix Technologies, Inc., Houston, Texas. We are quoting from their document as follows:

Part One: Brain Nutritional Deficits
Historically, people believed that alcoholism was caused by lack of willpower; that any "straight thinking" person could

control his/her drinking habit; and that failure to do so was a sign of weak character.

Now, as a result of scientific studies over the past 20 years, we know that these beliefs are wrong. There are at least three factors that appear to cause alcoholism—genetics, stress, and chronic alcohol abuse. These factors produce a deficiency that results in a disturbance in brain chemical signals. This causes well known physical and mental symptoms. These symptoms commonly include craving—often irresistible craving—for alcohol.

To understand this present view of alcoholism you have to understand something of how the brain regulates behavior. If the body signals the brain that a need exists, the brain responds by releasing chemical signals (messengers or transmitters) which cause an action to fill that need. Two such chemicals the brain normally produces are called endorphins and enkephalins. These two chemicals seek out and attach to mating receptors in the brain. The receptors accept only those chemicals whose molecules have the right (mating) shape. It is like a key (the chemical messenger) fitting into a lock (the receptor).

If a sufficient number of the receptors are filled with endorphins and enkephalins, you feel a sense of well-being (see figure 1). This is a natural sequence: the production of endorphins and enkephalins and the filling of the receptors, followed by a feeling of well-being. As long as those receptors are filled by endorphins and enkephalins, you feel well.

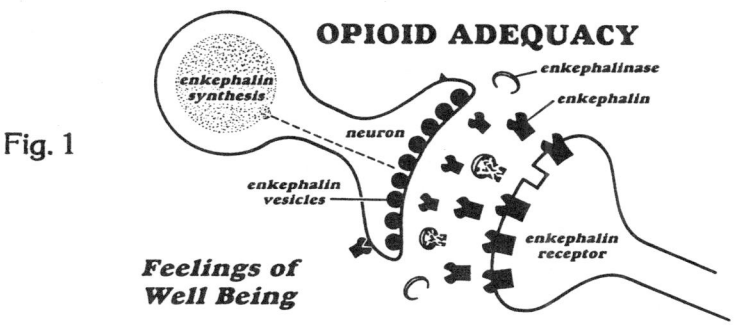

Fig. 1

But, if for some reason endorphin and enkephalin availability is reduced, and too few receptors are filled, the deficiency causes you to feel a sense of urgency and irritation (see figure 2). Similarly, if production is too high and an excessive number of receptors are filled, you feel a sense of euphoria that may be followed by a letdown. This, too, is natural, and is a major cause of the "ups and downs" of everyday life for most people.

Fig. 2

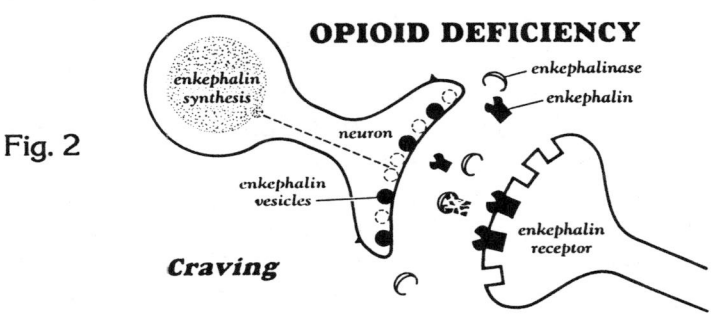

If you consume a drug such as morphine or heroin, these drugs take the place of endorphins and enkephalins at the receptors and, if taken in quantity, activate a large number of receptors and thereby create an unnatural euphoria. You feel "great" for a time, but the drug has a serious side effect: it causes the body to shut down production of natural endorphins and enkephalins. Then, as the drug wears off, your feeling of need becomes greater than ever. If drug consumption continues over a long period of time, the ability of the body to produce endorphins and enkephalins is reduced, and you become increasingly dependent upon the drug.

Alcoholism is not a single disease. Scientists believe that the deficits that result in changes in brain chemical transmitters may be arrived at by three pathways: 1) alcohol toxicity, alcohol induced or intensified alcoholism, where too much social drinking causes alcoholism; 2) stress, occupational or situational alcoholism, and 3) genetic predisposition, i.e. familial alcoholism.

Alcohol has recently been found to cause production of chemicals called tetrahydroisoquinolines (TIQ's), which have effects that resemble morphine and heroin. That is, they fill enkephalin receptors, produce an unnatural euphoria, and reduce the output of the natural endorphins and enkephalins (see figure 3). Because of this third effect, long-term use of large amounts of alcohol produces a permanent, urgent need for alcohol—the craving familiar to every alcoholic. As output of natural endorphins and enkephalins is reduced, the craving overcomes will power and becomes the dominant force in the person's life (see figure 4).

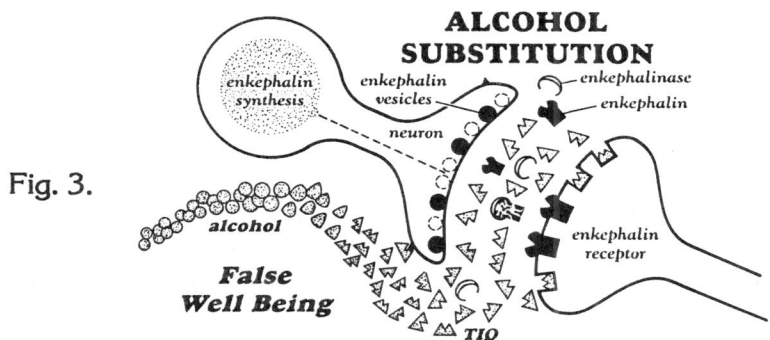

Fig. 3.

ALCOHOL SUBSTITUTION

enkephalin synthesis

enkephalin vesicles

enkephalinase

enkephalin

neuron

alcohol

enkephalin receptor

False Well Being

TIQ

The most recent research indicates that genetic factors are a major predisposing element in alcohol craving. It is thought that in genetically predisposed humans, from birth, the production of endorphins and enkephalins in the brain is abnormally low, and the resultant feeling of need and lack of fulfillment make such people susceptible to the illusory "highs" of drinking. Once the drinking habit is formed, the already low level of endorphins and enkephalins falls lower and lower, and dependence on alcohol becomes intense.

Stress leads to a reduction of enkephalins and endorphins. Alcohol, by producing TIQ's, can lead to stress reduction. Frequent exposure to highly stressful circumstances can facilitate a habit and in conjunction with chronic alcohol use, result in a physical need (see figures 3, 4).

Social drinking can get out of hand if a too-great or too-frequent intake of alcohol results in too many receptors being filled by TIQ's for extended periods, and the normal output of endorphins and enkephalins is curtailed (see figures 3, 4). In this case a simple habit generates a physical need—which strengthens the habit—and worsens the need, and so on.

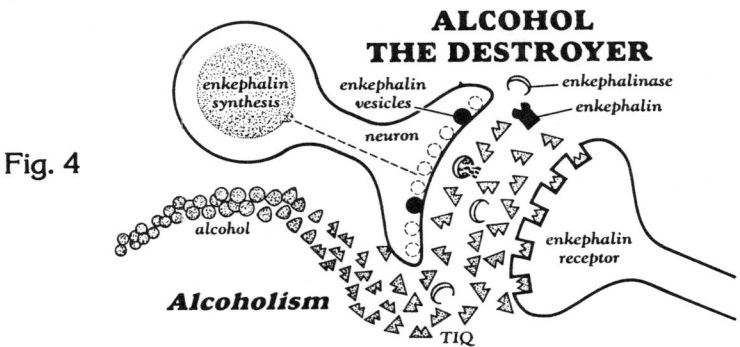

ALCOHOL THE DESTROYER

Fig. 4

Another group which exhibits certain dysfunctional behaviors, which may have a genetic basis, is the Adult Children of Alcoholics (ACA's). It is estimated that there are 28 million ACA's in the U.S. Scientists believe that this high risk population has distinct differences in their ability to metabolize alcohol, and in their response to alcohol. Many ACA's clinically have difficulties which include a high degree of stress and anger; insomnia; depression; and, compulsivity.

Part Two: Alcoholism and Nutrition

It has been observed that the above behaviors can be influenced by dietary supplementation of various amino acids and vitamins.

It is now well known that several amino acid neurotransmitter chemicals are reduced in the brain by alcohol. Among these are dopamine (a key substance for reward), serotonin (a substance related to sleep), GABA (a substance related to anxiety), norepinephrine (a substance related to depression), and enkephalins (substances related to craving).

By use of a nutritional approach, brain chemical messengers, which are known to be deficient in alcoholics, may be restored by selectively providing the body with specific amino acids and nutritional supplement vitamins (see figures 5, 6).

Fig. 5

Fig. 6

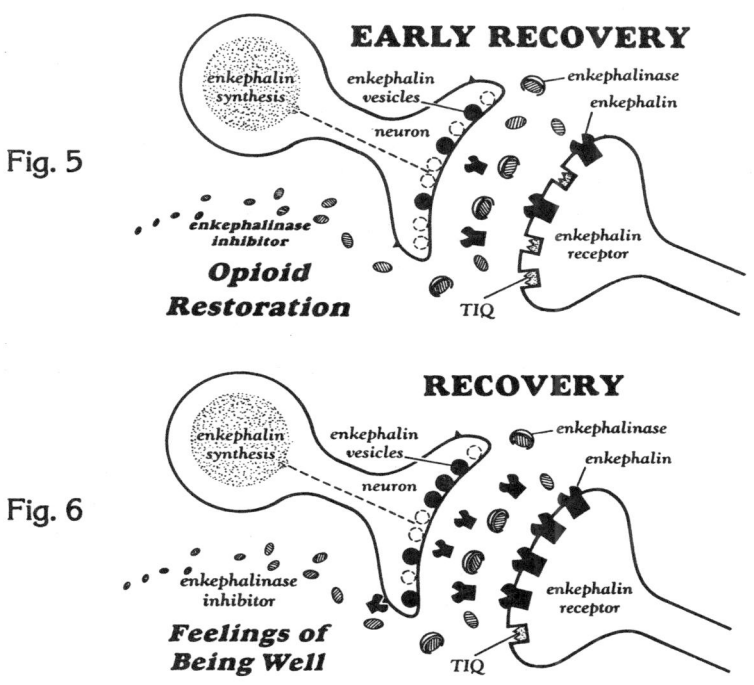

Amino acids which in special combinations have been reported to be helpful in restoring the alcoholic's brain nutritional balance include: L-tyrosine, DL-phenylalanine, L-glutamine, L-tryptophan [Since this information was written, L-tryptophan was taken off the market], and B-complex vitamins. It is important to note that numerous other nutritional deficiencies may also exist in alcoholics. These deficiencies are best overcome through proper diet and balanced nutrition and vitamin and mineral supplements.

We thank Drs. Blum and Trachtenberg for sharing the results of their research and for developing supplements designed to help alcoholics and other addicted people overcome their physical and chemical imbalances.

Allergy can also be a cause of alcoholism, constituting a fourth pathway to alcoholism. Earlier, we pointed out that people often crave what they are allergic to. An allergy to corn can reinforce a person's addiction to bourbon. An allergy to potato can reinforce addiction to vodka. A person allergic to grapes might favor wine and brandy. An allergy to any grain can cause a specific craving for the associated alcohol. Such a paradoxical condition is based on the body learning to adapt to its reaction to the allergen, and then expecting it as a normal course of functioning.

Because an increasing number of people are alcohol sensitive, the Systemic Clinic in Austin, Texas, has pioneered the production of liquid homeopathic remedies in a non-alcohol base. Some people are so sensitive to the effects of alcohol and its sources, that even one drop can cause an allergic reaction or re-ignite an addiction.

All of the substances and behaviors discussed in this chapter are symptoms of addictions when the body expresses a strong desire for them. We have listed some of the damages that these substances and activities can cause to make the point that all of the energy impostors take a toll on a person's health. Hopefully, this discussion will discourage these uses and behaviors and lead to the recognition that the need for them is simply a symptom of a biochemical and bioenergetic imbalance. Finally, we hope to encourage people to seek those therapies best suited to correct the imbalances and restore natural balance. Such therapies are often called alternative therapy and include the sciences of homeopathy, herbology, acupuncture, and nutrition.

8

COMPULSIVE ACTIVITIES

COMPULSIVE WORKING

Low energy is ususally the result of nutritional deficiencies, weakened immunity, metabolic, and hormonal imbalance. Low energy can cause the need for hustle-bustle workaholic activity, because hyperactivity defeats the body's need to slow down, rest, and do nothing. In a state of low energy, slowing down is felt as extreme fatigue.

Workaholics often drive themselves in high gear to mask the underlying feeling of exhaustion. In reality, the workaholic is headed toward adrenal burnout, acidosis, and nervous breakdown. There is nothing wrong with hard work, but when it becomes the only thing that makes a person feel alive and worthwhile, then it is a warning that the person is burning the candle at both ends. It is here, at this point, that activity becomes an addiction.

Most people get caught up in the compulsive activity syndrome gradually. Their desire to succeed, their dedication to a cause, their wish to avoid participating in stressful family relationships, their need to prove themselves or get a business off the ground engage the body's glandular and nerve energy systems rather than its regular metabolic energy, which scientists call the Kreb's cycle.

The fatigue of the hard work is not solved by rest and relaxation, because there never is time. Instead, the fast work pace of the next day's activities provides a new shot of adrenaline, the fight or flight hormone. Consequently, the hyped-up feeling of activity—the pseudo energy—becomes the standard for feeling good.

Bryan Robinson in his book, *Work Addiction*, discusses work abuse as a serious compulsive disorder. He considers compulsive working every bit as ravaging and insidious as alcoholism, for example. And, he finds that work addicts have similar symptoms as alcoholics: denial, reality distortions, getting high from work, and family and friendship problems, as well.

Robinson's studies have shown that frequently work represents the drug of choice for many people who grew up in dysfunctional families, because excessive work helps to overcome emotional pain. In a way, their work is a medication for neglected inner feelings.

A valuable point made by Robinson concerns the applause accorded by society to overworking. Overwork is generally appreciated in the U.S. way of life and is consequently rewarded. For these reasons, work addicts find it harder to face their addiction and its consequences, such as broken families, reduced work effectiveness, and ultimately, serious health problems.

At the time of this editing, President George Bush's endorsement of David Souter as Justice of the Supreme Court is being sold to the public via Souter's workaholic lifestyle. The media's attempts to build our admiration of the man and our trust in him are based on the fact that "all he's done all his life is work." This exemplifies the U.S. admiration of the workaholic ethic.

Workaholics feel pretty good when they are working and lousy when they slow down. Also, after a keyed-up day, something is needed to help them slow down, oftentimes a cocktail or a sleeping pill. A sleeping pill may make a person sleep, but it does nothing about the body's acid pH, which prevents sleep, and the diseases that can result from such acidic pH, such as diabetes, osteoporosis, cancer, and sciatica, for example.

The daily zooming up and zooming down puts a lot of wear and tear on the nerves, and can lead to "nerve fray," or a lack of proper insulation in the myelin nerve sheath. Fatty acids make up this nerve sheath. It is not uncommon to find high cholesterol levels and triglycerides in the excessively hard workers. The low and high density lipids can be in a good ratio IF the diet and liver are healthy, but total cholesterol is often elevated to 235-285, perhaps as a buffer or braking system to the over-activated adrenal glands. Such a pattern is seen in novice workaholics before the damage is too great. After a year of workaholic stress, the LDL (low density lipids associated with cardiovascular disease) elevates, and the high cholesterol level becomes a danger to cardiovascular health and life.

While on the subject of cholesterol, most nutritionists know that the total cholesterol level being read in grocery stores, shopping malls, and discount stores is virtually a meaningless exercise as far as real cardiovascular health is concerned. The important factor is the ratio of cholesterol's components—the low density lipid to total cholesterol. With proper ratios, there is little danger of cardiovascular disease even if total cholesterol is 350! With a high LDL, however, cardiovascular disease is only a matter of time.

The compulsive activity addiction syndrome could explain why some people seem to seek stressful relationships and argumentative situations. The stimulation that anger affords keeps the energy system in high gear. Their righteous indignation makes these people feel better. Picking a fight with a spouse may actually help keep the compulsive activity person in high gear and help avoid the lethargy and depression which would occur if the system slowed down. It is something to think about.

People should realize that the price they pay to passionately compete and be successful should also include specific times of relaxation. Work hard, play hard, and rest easy! This is the ticket to handling success.

Single working parents often get into an over-activity situation particularly if they have a demanding career or are self-employed. They are especially susceptible to the quick energy fixes of other addictive substances. If you are in this category, create time and the means for a weekly massage. Follow the Pro-Vita! Diet to optimize nutrition. Use a balanced, low potency, multiple food supplement. Embrace the tenets of good health and avoid stimulants including sodas, pastries, coffee, and pekoe tea. Also avoid alcohol and marijuana as a way to relax after the rat race of the day. Instead, make your life work naturally so that it will work for you.

EXCESSIVE JOGGING

Excessive exercise can be quite stressful for the body. In fact, the greater the energy glands' exhaustion, the more meaningful the stressful exercise becomes to the person. The reason for this is that exercise temporarily increases the energy metabolism of the exhausted person. But without nutritional reserves in the body, exercise ends up taking more energy than it gives. This condition occurs because exercise tears down body tissue to produce energy.

This is not an argument against exercise. Just pay attention to how you feel. If life is hardly worth living when you miss a day of jogging, the exercise is probably an addiction that is selling you short in the long run. Otherwise you probably need more exercise than you are getting. Low-impact aerobics and swimming are the better forms of routine exercise, as are work-outs on rowing machines. These activities exercise both the upper and lower halves of the body.

Water-walking exercise is particularly good and was a favorite of the late Dr. Stuart Wheelwright. To do this, stand chest high in water and walk. Every movement is exaggerated by the resistance of the water. Take a frisbee in each hand, and move them through the water so there is maximum resistance. As a personal story: one afternoon, Dr. Shirley Yanta brought Stu Wheelwright and me several frisbees, and we worked out in the hotel pool—walking and pushing the frisbees under water. The exercise was thorough, relaxing, and worked both the upper and lower halves of the body aerobically without strain. Wheelwright predicted that this form of exercise would gain credence over the years.

Compulsive joggers seek the high that they get from the "breaking through the wall" endorphin release. As with all addictions, the body develops a tolerance, and the person must jog farther and farther to get the high. The excessive exercise causes wear and tear on ankles, knees, and ligaments; and, unless the Pro-Vita! Diet is followed, nutrients are lost, and quality proteins are not made available to replace what is used.

In clinical work with compulsive joggers who run ten miles a day, I have seen hard, stringy muscles, and nutrient-depleted bodies which the owners thought were in great shape, except for the lurking feeling of fatigue if jogging were missed. These bodies responded beautifully to reduced running distance, increase in the nutrient-glandular support, and following the Pro-Vita! Diet plan.

The belief that people are jogging their way to health is erroneous until a careful plan is followed, and the addictive qualities avoided. Diet, proper supplements, additional upper body exercise and rest are essential for good health. Too much, even of a good thing, is always detrimental. A lack of exercise and too much dependence on stimulation from exercise are both imbalanced states.

EXCESSIVE EJACULATION

First, let me acknowledge New Yorker Jon Harris who encouraged me to bring out this form of addiction when at first I was reluctant to do so. Since the first printing of this book, several men have gained better health by understanding this material.

Sperm is a vital body fluid. Many nutrients make up its medium, including a mineral in relative short supply in many men—zinc. Like giving too much blood, a person can also give too much sperm and thereby deplete nutritional and bioenergetic reserves.

Hormones produced by the testes are vital to maintain good health, a strong immune system, proper pH (acid/alkaline balance), and strong adrenal and thyroid glands. Common problems associated with excessive ejaculation include sleepiness, inability to sleep without masturbation, loss of sex drive, baldness in some people, impotence, weak immunity, soft erection, prostate disorders, and exhaustion. This discussion is not a case for abstinence which is not healthy either, because prostate disorders can be caused both by overuse and abstinence. Instead, this information represents a message to watch the frequency of ejaculation, and to pay attention to how great the need for it is.

Few men realize that ejaculation can be both psychologically and physiologically addicting. The body experiences a momentary surge of energy, which may be followed by a low or sleepy period. This meets our definition of energy addiction on all three points—stimulation, gratification, weakening.

Orgasm releases endorphins which are brain chemicals that temporarily provide a feeling of well-being. In some people, the temporary stimulation is replaced by a lack of endorphins known as post-coital depression. Consequently, the need for more frequent stimulation becomes a driving force.

At what point does ejaculation become excessive? The answer has to be that it varies from person to person, and that it becomes more important with age. To evaluate the possible stress caused by ejaculation, sclerology is a valuable tool. A stress line could be found in the testes or prostate zone of the white areas of the eyes many years before a serious problem develops, even years before an indicator would appear in the iris. However, the feet would provide the first clue of stress, and a reflexologist would find tender points on the inside of the ankles.

In acupuncture it is taught that excessive masturbation leads to kidney weakness, because of the drainage of ch'i energy. One of the factors contributing to the problem is the lack of a partner, or the balancing energy. This concept stems from the principles of yin and yang, and suggests that masturbation is more energy-depleting than an orgasm with a partner to balance the energy flow.

This information is presented as something to think about, since the general consensus in Western thought is that there is no such thing as an energy discharge, or nutrient depletion when ejaculating. Another concept that is foreign to Western men is that an orgasm can be experienced without ejaculation. If a person were to develop this ability, there would be the pleasure without the loss of fluid, or fluid loss would be less frequent.

A patient once commented: "Sex is an energizing experience when it's right, depleting when it's wrong. What a blessing it's been to get this part of my life worked out."

LOUD ROCK 'N' ROLL MUSIC

William Congreve wrote in his book *The Mourning Bride* (1697) that music could "soothe the savage beast." There is no doubt that some music can do this. But there is another side to the coin. Loud music, particularly if featuring electric bass and rock 'n' roll rhythm with the accent on every third beat, stimulates the thyroid and adrenal glands, thus causing a faster metabolic rate. Many studies have shown that hard rock music kills plants, and weakens connective tissue in the body. But here is a new twist: some people get pseudo energy from rock 'n' roll stimulation, particularly when played at a low volume.

You may have heard that alpha waves are predominant in the brain in a state of relaxation and increased awareness. Scientists have also discovered other waves, such as beta, delta, and theta waves. Beta waves are disruptive to cellular activity. Yet, betas are the predominant waves emitted by electric rock 'n' roll and by other varieties of music to a lesser extent as well. Certain jazz, reggae, and soul songs carry a strong beta wave transmission, but this varies from song to song. In contrast, rock 'n' roll music consistently emits beta waves. Jazz comes in a distant second place with beta emissions. Other types of music feature occasional beta waves.

Music can increase the heartbeat and cause the release of endorphins in the brain. Music, or organized sounds, has the power to heal or cause weakness. The English pop star, Kate Bush, sings a song about military research "for a sound that can kill someone." Music can carry both positive and negative subliminal suggestions. The message here is discrimination. Be aware of the power of music, and pay attention to its effects.

This does not mean that a person cannot enjoy all kinds of music. But if you require doses of rock 'n' roll to make you feel alright, recognize it as a symptom of low energy and weak nerves. Stabilize your energy system with nutrition. This will also help minimize the negative effects of disruptive music when you do listen to it.

Since many people live in a perpetual state of over-excitement through job pressure, media blasts, and news addiction, highly stimulating music may only contribute to the eventual breakdown of health. Therefore, if you love loud hard rock music, you might occasionally choose music that helps to soothe and calm. You will enjoy it and benefit from it. You might try Pachebel's *Cannon in D Major,* or Wagner's *Prelude to Lohengrin,* or Ralph Vaughan Williams' *The Lark Ascending,* or Beethoven's *Pastoral Symphony,* or Satie's *Gymnopedie,* or music by Mozart, or countless other pieces that provide a beneficial delta wave form for balancing music impulses. Many other cultures feature music enriching the beneficial delta and theta waves in the human bioenergetic field.

The purpose of this section is not to criticize a particular form of music. People have criticized rock 'n' roll since its beginning, and have thereby only strengthened its popularity. When Neal Young sings that "rock 'n' roll will never die," he is probably right in a certain sense. As long as people need this music to feel better from an outside source, musicians will sing it.

I want to point out that Igor Stravinski's *The Rite of Spring,* which is often played on the classical music radio stations can be disruptive to certain brain patterns also. This does not make the music piece good or bad, it just means that music can be a catalyst for change. If someone is mentally unbalanced, Stravinski might be aggravating. To someone stymied in routine, this music might be the impulse that helps initiate transformation. We are simply discussing music from a bioenergetic perspective here without attaching any value judgements to it.

Sound patterns have a powerful influence on people. Music affects the body and arouses the emotions. On the physiological level, loud rock 'n' roll elevates the blood pressure, increases the heart rate, and can raise cholesterol levels, constricts the stomach and esophagus, dialates the pupils, and drives blood to the internal organs. This reaction is identical with the effects of stress and anxiety syndrome. It definitely affects the body, and adaptation can be habit-forming.

Music does not really qualify as an addiction, but it can be habit forming and people can become compulsive about needing it. We've discussed rock 'n' roll because it is the most physical music and it is played at a loud volume. Country and Western music can be just as habit forming if a person locks in on the emotions it evokes.

The key is to understand what our preferences in music are telling us. Then we stay in control and do not unwittingly become the effect of a negative feed-back loop—one which holds us or locks us into repeating a certain emotional pattern over and over.

To summerize, music's effects on the physical, emotional, and mental dimensions of a person can become compulsive or habit forming. Some people require music to get energy. They often turn on loud rock 'n' roll music to get revved up. Others require music to evoke an emotional state. They often listen to sad songs to mull over their disappointments. And others use music to escape from reality, to avoid confrontation with life.

To close this discussion on rock 'n' roll as a potential compulsive activety and thus an addictive symptom, here is a letter I'd like to share from a college student.

Dear Jack,

Since writing is how I clear my thoughts, I'm sending you this letter to mark a change for the better.... When I first read the part in *Energy & Addictions* on rock 'n' roll music, I thought it was absurd. I also thought you were just being stuffy like my parents about the type of music I like to listen to....but I began to pay attention and saw that what you said might be true.

After staying up late at a party, I wake up really tired. I can turn on my stereo, play rock 'n' roll loudly, and it is like a cup of coffee. It gets me going and off to class.

So I began to pay attention to the times I like to blast the radio in my car, or play my stereo real loud. It's always when I'm a little tired, like after a test.

Unfortunately, I saw I was doing this a lot. I'd bought a Walkman so I could play tapes between classes. I have to admit that I really do feel better after loud music.

So, three weeks ago, I came by your clinic and got the thyroid, adrenal, and nerve formulas you recommended. I cleaned up my diet. What a difference!

Now I have good energy all the time and I don't need rock 'n' roll to feel good. Of course, I still like my favorite songs, but I don't NEED the music, I just enjoy it.

When you autographed your book for me, you wrote "Always seek the true values in life," and that's exactly what I'm doing. Thanks to your help, I'm staying healthy.

C. S. Austin, Texas

9

HARD POISONS: COCAINE

This chapter about cocaine is included in the book because cocaine and the related substance crack are increasingly used in our society, often with deadly consequences. Since the basic information on the effects of cocaine is similar to that about other hard drugs, and since cocaine use is more prevalent, we will focus on this hard drug and not deal with other types to any great extent. Once the principles of addiction are understood, it does not really matter what the name of the drug is. With the era of designer drugs upon us, we find that new drugs can be created by simply altering a molecule. And each new drug will feature a slightly different characteristic in its primary effect as well as its side effects.

In the following discussion we are able to share with you the information which resulted from the research performed by Kenneth Blum, PhD, Michael C. Trachtenberg, PhD, and Laurel A. Loeblich, PhD. It should be noted that Dr. Blum is Chief of the Division of Alcohol and Substance Abuse at the University of Texas Health Science Center in San Antonio, Texas. We thank the researchers for allowing us to reprint the following information:

Some Things You Should Know About Cocaine

Introduction. Scientists test the benefits and/or destructive consequences of humans taking certain drugs by giving these drugs to animals with similar tissues, chemistry, etc. The results of many such experiments reveal that COCAINE IS MORE ADDICTING THAN HEROIN AND MORE LETHAL. The ultimate consequence of unlimited cocaine access in animals is always DEATH! In experimental animals allowed to self-administer the drug no more often than every 50 seconds, all die within 30 days. MONKEYS ALLOWED TO

SELF-ADMINISTER EVERY 10 SECONDS DIE WITHIN 5 DAYS.

The recent popularity of cocaine abuse might thus seem surprising. However, public awareness of scientific studies is slow and the profits from the sale of cocaine are so large that nearly any sales technique is tried. In the end it all boils down to the cocaine dealer's promise to his prospective customer, "It feels great, and you can use it occasionally—it really isn't addictive unless you're one of those idiots who allow themselves to get hooked on it." With this statement he is setting his trap. The very first 'hit' causes changes that lead to physical addiction as we will see below. And, of course, he never mentions the problems that usually develop, often after minimal usage of the drug. Common among these are:

- Sleeplessness
- Reduction in feeling pleasure from everyday experiences
- Increased number of accidents
- Poor appetite
- Depression
- Fatigue
- Suicidal thoughts
- Paranoia
- Reduced sexual performance
- Brain hemorrhages
- Lung hemorrhages
- Seizures
- Degenerated value system
- Loss of self esteem

Cocaine use is VERY dangerous. It can, and often does, cause heart attacks, seizures, and/or convulsions. Increasing the amount, using more frequently, and smoking and/or injecting instead of snorting all dramatically increase risk; these serious consequences can occur with even first time use. Cocaine is potentially lethal.

The deadliness of cocaine has radically increased during the last decade as more pure and therefore stronger cocaine has become available. This has been coupled with the increased effect obtained by new methods of administration, such as shooting (intravenous injection), freebasing (smoking crack), etc. While some people can 'snort a line' of cocaine occasionally in a 'recreational' manner, many are unable to stop there. The occasional lines become the weekly lines, which become the daily lines. All too often this leads to smoking or shooting cocaine in an effort to achieve a faster, bigger 'high'. The highly predictable end result has been well demonstrated in a large series of studies. It is virtually impossible to stop—often after only one such 'fast track' use. Inevitably the cocaine ends up in control of the person, instead of the person being in control of the use of the drug. Even worse, LESS than one third of those who are addicted can stop even with the aid of standard drug abuse treatment. New developments have given hope to most of the remaining two thirds. To understand how these work, we must first understand how cocaine acts on the brain.

The Chemistry of Cocaine

Cocaine is a naturally occurring stimulant derived from the leaves of the coca plant. The leaves contain only about one-half of one percent pure cocaine. Unlike pure cocaine, coca leaves contain a variety of minerals and vitamins. These nutrients are believed to chemically reduce the toxic effects of the cocaine contained in the leaf. When a leaf is chewed, a relatively modest amount of cocaine is released. Only a small quantity of that released is absorbed by the digestive system, and the digestion of it is very slow. For these reasons, the South American habit of chewing coca leaves has never become the serious public health problem associated with more potent forms and more efficient routes of administration.

In contrast the situation is dramatically changed when pure cocaine is used. If the substance is injected or smoked, the stimulating effects and feelings of euphoria are greatly magnified. Using cocaine in this way delivers significant amounts of the substance to the brain in seconds.

Once in the brain, cocaine acts upon the 'reward/punishment' (r/p) systems. The normal function of these systems is to encourage the individual to do, or not to do, specific things. For example, if the body requires a particular nutrient, a specific brain chemical will be put into 'short supply', causing the individual to feel ill at ease or have an urgent sense that something must be done. On the other hand, if the individual has just done something that was good for the body, release of certain brain chemicals will give the individual a sense of euphoria or elation. For example: the runner's high becomes encouragement to do further exercise. It also eases the muscle pain of hard work.

The mechanism by which the above takes place involves brain chemicals, called neurotransmitters. Cocaine's extraordinary release of one such chemical, dopamine, causes us to focus on this action.

The brain usually stores just enough dopamine to meet normal demands. For most people this supply needs only to be rebuilt slowly with small quantities of dopamine. Not much is needed as release of even small amounts for short periods of time causes a strong effect. For instance, during the sexual climax a small dopamine release over a fraction of a second gives a very powerful reward feeling. Cocaine causes a much larger release over a much longer period of time. This 'feels so good' that one can become 'hooked' after the first use. This is especially true of the first use of crack or shooting up. With repeated use of cocaine, the dopamine supply becomes depleted because it cannot be replenished quickly enough.

An analogy is helpful. The dopamine releases discussed above might be thought of as coming from a dam holding back a lake of dopamine. Normal use is rather like an occasional hole, the size of a toothpick, punched into the dam. The puncture releases a small amount of dopamine and then seals itself shut. The supply thus lost is replaced by a small trickle of dopamine coming from the cells which produce it. These cells could produce much more except that the 'raw materials' (precursors) they use are just sufficient for the need.

Snorting cocaine is analogous to firing a bullet through the dam with a pistol. It releases a much larger amount than the toothpick and the feeling of euphoria is very desirable.

However, the system is now depleted and rebuilding the supply to normal levels can take days from just one such use.

Smoking or shooting cocaine is analogous to firing a cannon through the dam. A great hole is breached causing profound euphoria. This feeling is so 'incredibly good' that almost no one can do it just once; in short, a person can become addicted after the first use. Needless to say, the dopamine supply after such use is greatly diminished and after many such uses no amount of cocaine will produce the good feeling.

It should be noted that too much cocaine can be fatal. Thus, if the first time user takes the large dosage required by the longer term user, his first use can be his last!

The cocaine abuser experiences three stages of drug effects:

1. The first is acute intoxication (whether from snorting, injecting, or smoking). For a short time there is less anxiety, more self-confidence and alertness, a perception of clearer vision and understanding, and increased sexual appetite. However, the experience may be marred by sexual indiscretions, irresponsible spending, and accidents attributable to reckless behavior.

2. Next the 'crash' replaces euphoria with longer term feelings of anxiety, fatigue, agitation, irritability, and depression. Perhaps worse, suicidal thoughts often increase during this stage. The abuser now faces three choices:1) suffer through this time, 2) take more cocaine to alleviate the 'crash', or 3) take another euphoriant drug which is less expensive,such as alcohol, marijuana, amphetamines, heroin, etc. This is how many cocaine abusers develop dependencies on other drugs. Most often alcohol is chosen as it is inexpensive, legal and often has been used before the cocaine addiction. Use of alcohol frequently leads to the cocaine abuser also becoming or intensifying his/her alcoholism.

3. Then the withdrawal stage follows—a lengthy period of limited ability to derive pleasure from normal activities. In long term cases, the abuser may permanently lose this

ability. At the same time a craving develops for the euphoric effects of cocaine. These cravings are usually satisfied by using the drug again; and thus, the addiction develops.

The Development of Cocaine Addiction

If cocaine use is repeated often, the resultant large and continuing dopamine releases cause a depletion of the dopamine supply. It also places a strain on the dopamine producing cells and abuses the dopamine release system. This is why many cocaine users report that "the first hit is by far the best." As further use is made of cocaine, the individual needs more and more just to get a desirable effect. Ultimately, the dopamine supply may become so small that cocaine "just doesn't give an acceptable hit."

At this point, the cocaine abuser will often decide to seek treatment. If so, he has made a fortunate decision. If he does not seek treatment he will then typically turn to other drugs to try to get the relief he needs. Often the new drug of choice is alcohol. As it produces artificial euphoriants, there is no dependence on naturally produced neurotransmitters. Consequently, the high can be easily obtained whenever it is desired and for as long as desired.

Unfortunately, the continual use of alcohol reduces the body's ability to produce the natural opioid. It is a process rather like muscle atrophy; any muscle which goes unused for long periods of time deteriorates and ultimately ceases to function. If the brain is no longer called upon to make the natural euphoriants (enkephalins and endorphins [opioids]) because substitutes are being supplied in the form of drugs, its ability to make the opioids deteriorates. When the cocaine abuser switches to alcohol or some other drug, his dopamine supply is given a chance to rebuild. Once it is rebuilt the addict sooner or later learns that cocaine will work again. Perhaps not as well as before, but at least acceptably. The cycle is then repeated. Each time, new damage is done to the body, especially the brain, and the likelihood of return of full mental and physical capacity is reduced even further.

Again, the frequent result is that the cocaine abuser also becomes an alcoholic or intensifies his/her alcoholism.

Pretreatment

At some point in time, before cocaine kills him the abuser MAY decide that he wants to stop. Although he can sometimes be helped to that decision through intervention, ultimately THIS IS A DECISION ONLY HE CAN MAKE. NO ONE ELSE CAN DO IT FOR HIM OR FORCE HIM TO IT.

The addict with a desire to stop using has several problems which must be solved simultaneously.

1. The physical problems mentioned above require medical treatment. Until they are treated, the now malfunctioning reward/punishment systems cause such extensive misdirection that very few addicts are able to stop using the cocaine, alcohol, etc., that will relieve the craving, depression and discomfort of withdrawal for at least a little while.

2. The long term use of cocaine, alcohol, etc. causes a strong psychological dependence upon them. When the abuser is depressed, he takes the drug. When the abuser is under stress, he takes the drug. When the abuser wants company, he calls a friend to share the drug. When the abuser feels incompetent, he takes the drug to 'make him feel more efficient.' And in general, when anything in his life could be better, he turns to the drug instead of attempting to work out the problem.

    Cocaine users have other behavioral patterns which are very difficult to break. The sight of white powder, a place where cocaine is purchased, or even a handful of cash may trigger a strong craving. These triggers may take a lifetime to overcome.

    Breaking the psychological dependencies takes professional counseling and long term help from support groups.

3. The abuser's social life revolved, perhaps for years, around people who abuse the same or similar substances. His entire social outlook and environment and perhaps even his work environment must now be changed. For

every loss that is felt—friends, social activity, job, etc.—a replacement must be found.

In the long term this may be the most difficult of the three. Even though the physical problems have been successfully set aside and the craving brought under control, if one's friends and associates use these substances, the recovering abuser will often be seduced into re-joining them. He will feel intimidated and coerced by his friends that are still using cocaine. Each of these friends HAS to convince himself, and every one around him, that he is not addicted. He believes that he can use the drug on a recreational bases. He MUST believe this, even though he may be using the drug several times a day, every day! To not believe it is to accept that he is not in control, that the drug is controlling him and that he is powerless over the drug. Accepting this fact would mean that he would have to stop using the drug, a step he is as yet unwilling to consider. This scenario is the major symptom of this disease. It is called DENIAL!

Treatment

Traditional treatment of the physical problems has been to isolate the abuser in a hospital-like facility for three or four weeks. During this time the patient is treated psychologically for the cocaine addiction and advised to join a twelve step program, such as Cocaine Anonymous, Narcotics Anonymous, etc., for long term support. This general approach has been widely used and is responsible for the vast majority of treatment successes to date.

The basic disadvantage of this approach is that the six weeks to two months period during which the dopamine supply is being rebuilt is very stressful emotionally. This period of stress is extremely distracting. It does not allow the patient to properly concentrate or to have an accurate perception of what the psychological counseling is supposed to help him learn. This in combination with the ever present 'triggers' (e.g. white powders) usually leads back to cocaine abuse and then total relapse.

Recovery

The recovery problem is made more difficult by the fact that extensive cocaine use puts the metabolic system into a serious state of inefficiency. This greatly impairs the body's ability to use nutrients to make dopamine. Obviously, if the dopamine rebuilding time could be shortened, the patient would be able to take better advantage of the counseling he receives in treatment..

Fortunately, the dopamine production can be greatly augmented by considerably over-supplying the required nutrients. A closer look is needed to more fully understand this:

Amino acids are the building blocks (precursors) from which proteins and neurotransmitters, such as dopamine, are made. Amino acids are taken into the body in everyday foods. Usually there are just enough for the production of sufficient dopemine. However, for the cocaine addict, this supply is quite insufficient. Heavily supplementing the normal intake of amino acids ensures that they are never in short supply. And, fortunately, overproduction of dopamine does not occur if more precursors are supplied than can be used, as the body's 'production capacity' itself sets the limit on dopamine produced.

A useful analogy likens the chemical producing cells in the body to small factories. Raw materials (precursors) are delivered to the back door and customers receive the finished product at the front door. Thus, if the raw material is in limited supply, the production levels are set at something below 100% efficiency. (In the case of dopamine the normal level is less than 30%). By supplying all of the materials the factory can use, 100% efficiency can be achieved. But oversupplying can never cause 100% output to be exceeded.

Other amino acids are also needed in larger than usual quantities. These help in dealing with insomnia, craving and stress.

Further, as the cocaine addict's metabolic system is in serious dysfunction, he needs more of certain, specific vitamins and minerals than he would otherwise. In clinical studies cocaine addicts were found to be deficient in zinc, calcium, magnesium and many of the B vitamins.

Therefore, many modern treatment centers include in their therapy a patented, specially formulated, nutritional supplement designed specifically for the cocaine addict. This nutritional supplement helps to allow a patient to be alert, free of the insatiable NEED for cocaine, and willing and able to receive the counsel and support which are critical to recovery.

Conclusion

For the addict to rid himself of his cocaine addiction he must make the decision to take that very difficult first step toward recovery and then to continue on that path. The way is not easy, but it is CRITICALLY worthwhile.

It is important to remember the words of those who have been successful in the past, "First you must WANT TO 'GET CLEAN'—others wanting it for you doesn't help. Once you truly have the desire to get clean, YOU CAN, BUT YOU NEED HELP. And, you can get that help from your doctor, through his/her recommendations, your counselor, through his guidance, and from a support group which they recommend to you."

10

HOW TO STOP SMOKING
WHY DO PEOPLE SMOKE EVEN THOUGH IT'S DETRIMENTAL TO HEALTH?

The following discussion originates from a lecture given in February, 1986, in Austin, Texas. In this presentation we look at the the addictive process in general, and examine specifically the global affliction of smoking. Whether you smoke or not, there should be interesting information here for anyone.

For many years, nutritionists, chemists, and doctors have pointed out the detrimental effects of tobacco on people's health. Nutritionists were the first specialists to teach that smoking tobacco lowers the body's vitamin C levels as much as 40%. During the last ten years, a great deal of research has been conducted on the beneficial role of vitamin C as protection against cancer, colds, flu, the aging process, cardiovascular disease, and immune deficiencies. And the information on vitamin C is only a very small part of the entire smoking picture.

Virtually every day brings new findings showing why people who smoke, or use other forms of tobacco, must stop, if they want to live a healthful life. This simple fact alone is reason enough to shun tobacco, and let it return to its more natural place in the herb kingdom to serve as a remedy to break excessively high fevers, to induce vomiting, and to act as an insecticide.

After all, no one wants to end life in a hospital, gasping for precious air, coughing up blood and writhing in pain, as tumors take over the life processes. Yet, in spite of the horror stories, threats, the Surgeon General's warning, and a thousand other logical and sound reasons for not smoking, people persist in crippling their lives with tobacco.

You might ask yourself: "Why? How could anyone in their right mind do such a foolish thing?" There are valid reasons for smoking. First of all, it helps some people feel better, because it helps them to cope with stress. Smoking also helps people to temporarily overcome depression. Tobacco is not the best, or the only, way to cope with stress or depression, but it is one temporary solution.

There are many other reasons why people learn to smoke. Psychiatry has explored the oral fixation angle which stems from a need to seek solace by nursing at the breast. Some people have a need to be accepted by a peer group which holds smoking in esteem. Others succumb to attractive advertising. And some people could not make it through a day without the stimulation of tobacco. Smoking keeps them going. The respected nutritionist, Dr. M.T. Morter, remarks that smoking makes people feel good while it is killing them. Morter's concept is a key to understanding the attraction of addictive activities.

Whatever may be the reason for an addiction, it is more powerful than logic.

Now, perhaps for the first time, you will learn about some of the metabolic, or physical energy, processes of the body, as well as the bio-energetic processes; and why there exists an addiction in the first place. You will also learn that nutrition plays a critical role in a person's ability to let go of smoking, as well as about nutrition's well-documented role in rebuilding damaged tissues. Also, you may find some compassion for people who still smoke, when you discover that using tobacco is only a symptom of nutritional/biochemical or attitudinal energy imbalances. And that tobacco is not simply a poisonous substance, causing ill health, used by irresponsible, weak-willed or self-destructive people.

Most people are not accustomed to viewing smoking as a SYMPTOM, because they only hear about it as a CAUSE of lung cancer, heart disease, hypoglycemia, chronic infections, emphysema, and so on. Therefore I want to repeat the following for emphasis: smoking, as well as chewing tobacco, is a symptom of a biochemical and bioenergetic imbalance either pre-existant or created by experimentation with tobacco, not just the cause of all the diseases we read about. As a symptom, it is no different than admitting that you are tired; or that you do not feel well; or that you are having difficulty coping with the pressure of living; or that you have an unfulfilled need for love.

Other symptoms of the same bioenergetic imbalance include dependencies on alcohol, coffee, tea, marijuana, chocolate, recreational drugs, and sugar. It is true that the use of such substances helped create the metabolic imbalance which then dictated continued use. But usually, there first existed nutritional (biochemical) and energy imbalances that provided the environment, or tendency, toward addiction.

People with nutritional imbalances have a much greater chance of tobacco addiction—as do those with hereditary endorphin, or brain chemical, imbalances—than those persons who have a stable nutritional and metabolic balance.

This means that if a healthy, nutritionally stable person were to try smoking, he or she would cough, choke, get nauseated, and probably leave it alone. Unless other pressures, such as peer acceptance, advertising role models, and adolescent striving for independence, encourage the individual to "learn" to smoke. Such a person does not have inherent, depressive tendencies or a biochemical imbalance.

However, when a person with nutritional, or energy, deficiencies and imbalanced brain chemistry smokes a cigarette for the first time, he or she coughs, chokes, and gets a little nauseated; but most importantly, this person gets noticeable adrenal gland stimulation, which provides a semblance of the inherent energy that is missing. The person thinks: "Hey, I got a buzz off that! A little dizzy, but more energy, and I feel better." Later, when the effect wears off, the body sends the message: "Let's try that again. I liked having that stimulation and endorphin release, and it also seemed to help me relax and cope." And so the addiction begins. And, as with so many addictive substances, smoking causes the need for further stimulation, because it now has created a further nutritional/energetic deficit. Also, since the emotional needs attached to smoking, such as self-image, and help with heartache, for example, were not resolved by tobacco, a repetition or escape is once again required.

If smoking is only a symptom, what is the real problem, the cause, and ultimately the solution?

This chart shows the role of nutrition in solving energy-addictions.

SYMPTOM = addiction to artificial stimulation (tobacco use).

CAUSES = lack of energy (metabolic imbalance, improper nutrition), and/or emotional difficulties, feeling inadequate (often a nutritional imbalance), low stimulus barriers in the brain, imbalanced brain chemistry. Imbalances make a person more susceptible to tobacco influences.

A SOLUTION = proper nutrition addresses major causes, because biochemical, energetic, and emotional imbalance are often nutrition-related. Nutrition can help reestablish the energy glands, normalize metabolic imbalances, stabilize brain chemistry, promote health, and minimize the effects of stress. Other holistic therapies (counseling or support groups) can help with emotionally based and co-dependency issues.

Of course, this symptom of tobacco use is reinforced by advertising, based on subliminal and need-fulfilling images, to encourage a person to continue trying cigarettes until the addictive process is complete. Such addictions are good for business.

Smoking becomes an addiction when the body metabolism depends on nicotine and cadmium (a toxic metal used in tobacco processing) for energy and brain chemistry stimulation. Clever advertising encourages a person to continue smoking by portraying positive and reinforcing images, such as the rugged Marlboro Man; the seductive, yet feminist, Virginia Slims woman; various clean and refreshing activities; and happy relationships. Subliminal images are frequently used to register the smoking attraction deep within a person's subconscious mind. For example, the camel-man, used on many different billboards to advertise Camel cigarettes, resembles a penis and scrotum, and thus strikes an archetypal chord with its subliminal message. These media images strike deeply into the subconscious mind and therefore program the susceptible person to smoke.

Smoking provides a temporary lift in energy by stimulating the energy glands, both the adrenal and thyroid glands. People, whose energy glands are weak, tend to smoke for the artificial stimulation. In essence, they are providing an energy source to their bodies. But like having to work all day to afford labor-saving appliances that break down, this type of energy source costs more than it is ultimately worth, primarily because it weakens the immune system, and because it leads to degenerative diseases.

Why a weakened immune system? Because the adrenal glands act in opposition to the thymus gland, the major immune system regulator. When the adrenal glands are secreting the high energy hormone adrenaline, or the anti-inflammatory hormones like cortisone, then the thymus function is greatly reduced. Consequently, the immunity to disease is diminished. The additional burden of some 2,000 chemicals from smoke cause more challenges to the immune system. For this reason, smokers are more susceptible to infections, candida, and other immune deficient diseases. Such conditions are all a perfectly normal reaction of the body. When fight or flight adrenaline rules the metabolism, the body's attention is on physical survival. The immune system and the toxin-removing lymphatic system become subordinated to the single purpose of staying alive via adrenal response. Also, liver function becomes impaired, and the liver is one of the most important organs in the body. For more information on the liver see the book, *The Liver Triad* (Tips, 1989).

When startled, frightened or surprised, people often say: "My heart skipped a beat." This reaction refers to the thymus, or heart-center energy vortex, which is instantly affected. This stimulation is one reason why people like scary or suspenseful movies. Such films play on the endocrine hormones, thus altering the day-to-day homeostasis, or metabolic balance, of the body. This is also why loud rock 'n' roll music is listed as an energy-addictive activity because it can alter the hormonal functioning of the body. Also, the flashing lights synchronized to rock music and used in discotecs are effective manipulators of the thyroid, adrenal, and thymus glands.

The words "artificial stimulation" were used earlier, because smoking harnesses the wrong energy system through non-genuine means. The following represents an analogy. Suppose that you want to run a car at 30 mph, but the transmission slips, and the car only moves at 15 mph. So you engage the turbocharger and force the engine to race, and with this enormous outburst of energy you get the car up to 30 mph, despite the slipping transmission.

The turbocharger worked, but it is the wrong energy system. Fixing the transmission would provide the proper energy system to attain 30 mph. The turbocharger effect is very similar to what smoking does to the body. Smoking races the adrenal medulla (adrenaline-producing part) and cortex (cortisol-producing part) to exhaustion.

Nicotine, and the toxic metal cadmium, stimulate the adrenal medulla to produce adrenaline, a hormone normally reserved for life and death, fight or flight situations. Adrenaline raises blood pressure, accelerates heart rate, causes sugar to be released into the bloodstream, and expends a great deal of energy. Constant stimulation can burn out the adrenal glands, just like excessive use of a turbocharger can burn out an engine. Burned out adrenals result in fatigue and a craving for artificial stimulation, such as smoking, use of alcohol, refined sugars, and drugs. It is worth noting here that marijuana contains twenty times more cadmium than tobacco. This fact could well imply that a need for marijuana is more than psychological, although for years medical science classified marijuana as non-addictive.

In addition to providing a mild stimulation, nicotine acts as a brain chemical to provide a barrier against too much stimulation. This stimulus barrier helps some people to focus on the task at hand, and it provides relief from the stress of too much input to the brain. Nicotine is an example of a drug that helps people to cope with a brain chemical deficiency and to feel better, while at the same time, it is killing them.

For a stop smoking program to be successful, safe and lasting, there are three major areas that should be addressed: 1) a new behavior pattern, both physical and emotional, needs to be established; 2) stress must be managed; and 3) nutrition should be optimal. This discussion focuses on nutrition, and on some of nutrition's interrelationships with behavior and stress as well.

Nutrition can help supply natural brain chemicals, so that artificial stimulus barriers are not needed. Nutrition can help with depressive tendencies. It can also help to detoxify and rebuild health. In short, nutrition offers a great deal in over-coming the addiction of smoking!

NEW BEHAVIOR PATTERNING

This topic deals with the behavior modification or B-Mod aspect of breaking addictions which a number of clinics use as part of their therapies.

The behavior pattern consists of repeated, ingrained acts or motor skills, such as tapping out a cigarette, rolling a cigar between the fingers, packing a pipe, pinching off a chew, and so forth. Such gratifying activities of tobacco use become associated with the relief and feeling better provided by a new shot of nicotine, and thus become a part of the whole process.

To reprogram these comforting and routine behaviors, a body requires nutrients and energy much the same way that reprogramming a computer requires electricity and the attention of a programmer. If the body's energy supply is linked to an addiction, and the energy materials are being supplied by repetitive movements, there is an additional obstacle to breaking the addiction —the neuromuscular engram—which means the brain/nerve-to-muscle habitual response pattern.

The behavior pattern simply refers to the ritual of an addiction. The brain recognizes the need for tobacco and sends out the signal to the muscular system to act. Being a faculty of habit, the brain programs the body's motions. People who always smoke after eating will have the greatest urge to smoke after each meal, even though they are trying to quit. This is the engram or habit, and its pattern runs right through the cells of the muscles required to perform the act of smoking.

If this idea sounds odd, consider that this concept is well-known in music. In addition to the brain, a pianist's fingers remember how to play the song after it has been rehearsed many times. This is called cellular memory.

The same is true for codependent relationships, incidentally. People choose the same relationship pattern over and over again. Even though the faces of the partners change, the same game is being played, and inevitably the same consequences are reaped—a poor, unfulfilling relationship.

With smoking, things like tapping the pack of cigarettes on the index finger, tapping the butt of the cigarette on the lighter to pack the tobacco tighter, and so forth, become a part of the addiction. The times of the day become part of the smoking pattern also: after the morning cup of coffee, after the mid-morning snack, upon completion of tasks at work, or after passionate experiences. These patterns become an enjoyable part of the entire addictive process.

The neuromuscular engram is made up of minerals and nucleoprotein patterns which are bioenergetically arranged. But the important point to understand is that these minerals and proteins form the cellular memory which is a part of the tobacco habit. Professionals often use behavior modification techniques to reprogram these patterns, so that they become uncomfortable rather than enjoyable patterns. Such techniques, for example, include shocking the person with low voltage upon exhibiting a certain behavior. There's nothing like the old cattle prod to help provide an attitude adjustment!

The vital question is: where does the body get the energy and raw materials (minerals and nucleoproteins), to alter the behavior pattern and break the habit? Minerals, obtained through the nutritive process of enzyme-rich foods, provide the electrolytes (electrically charged mineral particles) and other energy factors, such as the food's own bioelectrical pattern, needed as an energy source. The research in this field centers on the colloidal properties of minerals and the crystalline structure of water, and how they are the bits and bytes of our body computers. This represents a fascinating, highly technical area of research. The bottom line of these investigations is that behavior modification is much easier and more effective, when a proper mineral balance and readily available nucleoproteins exist. Proper mineral balance, to my knowledge, has never been found in a smoker. In fact, it is well documented that smokers have inverted and unbalanced mineral ratios. Hence the case for proper nutritional supplementation for more effective behavior modification, such as low potency, natural vitamins, enzymated minerals, and a protein-assimilable dietary pattern, as described in the book, *Pro-Vita! Diet* (Tips, 1989).

Clinically, we use the hair/tissue analysis, commonly known as a hair test, as a basis for understanding the body's mineral ratios, and how to apply nutritional and glandular support to help the body back to a more balanced level of health. The Amino Acid Profile from urine also provides important insights into what the body is doing to maintain the best health it can under the circumstances of nicotine drug poisoning.

NEW STRESS MANAGEMENT

The stress management part of breaking the addictive pattern relates primarily to physical stress and the body's ability to relax. Smoking is closely linked to taking a moment to relax and reflect, as is coffee drinking and marijuana use. Smoking fits into the pattern of how people cope with stress. The fact that it also CAUSES stress is separate from this role of apparent relaxation.

Since nicotine acts as a stimulus barrier in the brain, it assumes a position in the brain chemistry that gives the effect of helping calm people's nerves. For this reason, many people do not recognize tobacco as a stimulant. Instead, they are only aware of the calming and coping effect. Consequently, they do not realize how much of the need being fulfilled is actually energy-based.

The stimulus-barrier effect is analogous to having cotton in your ears, when the noise level is too high. This effect helps buffer the stimuli of sight, smell, taste, hearing, and touch to the brain, because it functions at a very high level already with so much media input, traffic noise, and chemicals in the air.

It is important to understand how the stimulus-barrier effect works, when on a program to stop smoking. When a person stops smoking, the nicotine-based stimulus-barrier will not be maintained, and the body will ultimately use it up and remove its by-products as toxins. In the transition or withdrawal period, frequent headaches can occur or an over-sensitivity to the environment. This happens because the brain lacks the nicotine-based stimulus barrier, and now must readjust its chemical balance to include the natural barrier process, based on acetylcholine.

This condition of headaches and sensitivities can be helped nutritionally with foods that provide the vitamin/lipid choline, such as egg yolk, cereals, fish, legumes, and lecithin. The brain derives the chemical acetylcholine from choline, which serves as the stimulus barrier that controls how much impact any outside stimulation has on the brain. Choline may substitute for nicotine in its role in brain chemistry without the side effects of nicotine. And as a healthful nutrient, choline plays several vital functions in the body chemistry, including maintaining the elasticity of membranes in the lungs, memory function, and nerve tissue structure.

People, in general, are stressed largely due to their pace of life, lack of exercise, and sensory bombardment through the media. Smokers are even more stressed and actively seek relief from the stress, usually in the harmful ways, which is largely due to ignorance of how the body derives energy from nutrition.

For this reason, it is often recommended for people to begin a mild aerobic exercise program or swimming, if they do not already participate in an exercise program or athletic activities. Notice the word "mild." There are many reasons why an exercise program for smokers must not be too strenuous, including their tendency toward cardiovascular weakness, damaged heart tissue, a lack of effective toxin elimination abilities, and a need to avoid excessive stress during the transition period. The benefits of the mild, but effective exercise include the mobilization of the lymphatic system to remove toxins from the body; the use of muscles which aids metabolic processes; the raising of body temperature which pasteurizes harmful bacteria and micro-organism; and improved circulation to the brain which is how the nutrients get there to help with overcoming the addictive process.

Herbs and nutrition have been found to be a great help in stopping smoking, because certain nutrients can help people relax, reduce the withdrawal jitters without a sedative effect, and detoxify the poisons in the bloodstream as they are being released. Nutrients can support the elimination organs (colon, kidneys, lungs, and skin), so that the pathways for detoxification do not become overburdened.

Another situation frequently occurs when smoking is discontinued suddenly. Since nicotine blocks stimulation of the brain—the soothing or relaxing aspect of smoking—when tobacco use is stopped suddenly, there is an overstimulation of the brain by things such as noise, light, and even touch. This causes a perception of great stress and irritability. Liquid lecithin, a nutrient known as a brain food, is often suggested to support this transition. Choline, a constituent of lecithin, is used by the brain to make acetylcholine which serves to regulate, or buffer, the intensity of outside stimulation. Liquid lecithin in capsules is best, since most granular lecithins have a rancid element in them. A steam-extracted lecithin is preferable, since it does not contain residues of the skelly oil, or kerosene-related solvents, used in the extraction process.

In addition to physical tension, stress also relates to the emotional and psychological gratification involved in oral stimulation which, together with relieving intangible stress, relieves physical stress. It becomes clear, that in addition to being a physical addiction, smoking is often an emotional addiction. People smoke to reduce frustration and to feel more loved, for example. This means that both physical and emotional needs are trying to be fulfilled through tobacco use. Nutritionists often recommend homeopathic flower remedies, such as the Bach Flower Remedies, the legacy of Dr. Edward Bach of England, to assist with the mental states associated with smoking.

Homeopathic remedies that can play a decisive role in breaking tobacco and other addictions include Ignatia Amara, Tobaccum, Lobelia Avenasativa, Coffea, Kali Phos, Nux Vomica, Daphne Indica, and Cactus Grand. These remedies need to be recommended by a practicing homeopath. The point here is that there are many viable, non-toxic supports available to help stop the use of tobacco.

Orthomolecular psychiatrists are medical doctors who specialize in vitamins and minerals and their role in mental and emotional health. Case histories and research show that many emotional and mental stresses are directly related to nutritional deficiencies and imbalances. Dr. Michael Lesser, M.D., points out that "tobacco, a stimulant, burns up thiamine, [a B vitamin, the lack of which] can cause depression, apathy, confusion, feelings of impending doom...." The connection between nutrition and many kinds of stress is well established. And regarding mineral balance, it is known that smoking elevates copper to abnormal levels. In turn, high copper is linked to schizophrenia, manic depression, epilepsy, hyperthyroidism, premenstrual syndrome, and many other detrimental conditions.

Consequently, nutrition plays an important role in reducing stress. Smoking destroys the very nutrients that protect the body from stress, yet it gives the appearance of helping a person to cope with stress by providing a temporary, and costly, form of energy and chemicals. This is one example why smoking, and any other addiction, is an energy impostor. As for dietary recommendations for stress, it can simply be said that alkalizing foods are the ones that heal. These foods are fresh fruits and vegetables that contain living enzymes.

Why a concern about foods that alkalize the body? Stress causes the release of acids from the cells. This can easily be measured with pH test paper. People who quit smoking should increase their intake of vegetables, and eat more fruit, if candida albicans, the yeast/fungus infection, is not a concern. Vegetables and fruits are nature's great alkalizers.

Another reason for eating alkalizing foods is that more nicotine and other poisons can be eliminated in an alkaline urine than in an acid urine. Alkalizing foods replenish much needed minerals, such as calcium, sodium, potassium, and magnesium. Some of the strongest alkalizing foods are lemons, limes, and figs. Carrot juice is a good alkalizer, but has a high sugar content. People often think of citrus fruits as acid foods. In fact, they are acid in the stomach, but alkalizing to the blood because the body easily breaks the acid bond, metabolically leaving an alkaline ash.

The key to alkalizing, or relieving the blood of excessive acids, is through enzymes because they are capable of neutralizing metabolic wastes. Enzymes such as protease, amylase, cellulase, lipase, peroxidase, maltase, oxidase, invertase, and phosphatase, can help correct an over-acid condition, if they are used together on an empty stomach.

There are two sides to the acid/alkaline issue, when considering the discontinuation of tobacco. If the urine is acid, fewer additional poisons can be eliminated at that time, resulting in prolonged effects of nicotine as a stimulus-barrier in the brain, or less need to smoke. However, alkalinity will allow more acids and toxins to pass through the urine, thus hastening the detox effort and ultimate freedom from the addiction. But with alkalinity withdrawal symptoms are more prominent, as the need for the body to change becomes greater.

When a person is ready to break through the smoking addiction, fresh lemon juice in water will help flush out nicotine and toxic residues, as will homeopathic and enzymatic support. Such natural therapies will further support the adrenals in their acid/alkaline regulatory function, and relieve tensions associated with an acid metabolism. Also, taking vitamin C, which is initially an acid, in therapeutic doses (3000 mg 2 or 3 times a day) causes an alkaline reaction, and can help flush out toxins.

The general dietary recommendation is to have one meal a day of only vegetables, both raw vegetables, like salads with leaf lettuce—but not head (iceberg) lettuce which contain opiates and retards bowel functions—and lightly steamed vegetables. For example: fresh garden salad prepared of several vegetables and a plate of lightly steamed broccoli, cabbage, new potatoes, and asparagus. A little water for a beverage, but no coffee, tea, or sodas. It is important to not make too many dietary changes at once, because too many changes will cause stress and failure. Just the one vegetable meal a day is a good start. It will provide significant impact without upsetting the system. This represents a tremendous step towards better health through nutrition.

RULE OUT CANCER

At the time a smoker decides to quit and embrace a more healthful life-style, it is a good idea to find out exactly how the lung's health is in regards to cancer. A simple test, a sputum cytology, can be performed by a lab.

The report will show the lung condition to be in a state of normalcy, inflammation, metaplasia, dysplasia (pre-malignant), carcinoma (in situ) or carcinoma (invasive). Clinically, it is best to know the results, either to put a person's mind at rest, or to get appropriate treatment.

Many smokers have an intellectual understanding of the health dangers of their habit, as well as a logical agreement that smoking costs a lot, smells bad, stains teeth, damages clothing, for example. But they fail to believe that there are detrimental effects to their own bodies. There is something about the human mind that wants to believe: "It happens to the other guy, but not to me."

Smoking damage occurs to EVERY smoker, AND to those who are in their proximity which we discuss shortly. Much of the damage caused by smoking is not irreversible. Nutrition is very successful in helping the body heal itself of damage.

It has been amusing to observe the recent implementation of the non-smoking laws. Naturally, there has been so much relief for nonsmokers. But now the tobacco interests want to sue for a loss of rights on behalf of smokers. It is high time to realize that smoke is body-invasive. As a child, after a scuffle with another child, I was sternly reprimanded by being told that "my rights end where the other guy's nose begins." This was an attempt to teach me that I had no right to punch someone in the nose. This should also hold true for smoke. People certainly can retain the right to poison themselves, but should not have a right to poison others via indirect smoke.

SMOKE AFFECTS NONSMOKERS

Research has clearly established that nonsmokers are greatly affected by tobacco smoke. Some smokers think that a little smoke will not hurt a nonsmoker, but they are irrefutably incorrect. In fact, smoke is more harmful to the non-smoker than to the smoker.

The reason for the harm caused by secondary smoke is that the smoker's homeostasis, or metabolic balance, is established to accommodate the perpetual supply of poisons. In other words, a smoker's body has adapted to its environment and, in certain respects, derives its functioning from tobacco toxin intake.

But this is not the case with the nonsmoker. The smoke hits this person with full impact, unexpectedly poisoning the nonsmoker's system. It is well documented that great harm has been inflicted upon nonsmokers who sit close to smokers in the workplace. The same harm is inflicted upon children whose parents smoke.

Most people would not want to deny a person their right to enjoy tobacco, but the strongest inalienable right must belong to the nonsmoker. Smokers might consider refraining from smoking in restaurants, and public places with the same courtesy they apply to passing gas. It is socially unacceptable to inflict the poisons of tobacco on children and non-smokers.

The medical establishment has proven that smoking damages the unborn child during its fetal development. This point is repeated here as a reminder for pregnant women who smoke and/or are in proximity to smokers. And it reminds of an anecdote. A six o'clock news interviewer spoke with a woman who was protesting against abortion. She was pregnant and smoking. It seems that her mindset was that it is wrong to abort a pregnancy, but alright to cause birth defects.

Since frequently smokers are unaware of the damage their smoke causes to nonsmokers—particularly the smoke that is not inhaled by the smoker—the nonsmoker might want to consider using an air purifier in the home or work area. There are a variety of air filters and air ionizers available. Our preference is for the high efficiency particle air filters, because they provide the cleanest air. They are not expensive, and they do not emit ozone as the negative ion generators do. Also, electronic precipitators make good air cleaners, though they require a little maintenance.

With rising concerns about airborne pollutants, including radiation, hydrocarbons, lead from gasoline, pollens, viruses, bacteria and parasites, a clean air device in the home, car, and workplace may become a health priority the way water purifiers, vegetable juicers, and nutritional supplements have become basic necessities for health-conscious people.

NUTRITION AND NUTRITIONAL THERAPIES

Good nutrition is doubly important for people who are quitting smoking. It replaces depleted vitamin, mineral, enzyme, and amino acid reserves that are basic to proper body function. Good nutrition also helps to reduce the stresses of the transition period. In other words, eating well makes quitting easier! And later, when a new homeostasis, or metabolic balance, is attained, nutrition provides the building blocks for repairing tissues damaged by smoking, i.e., lungs, throat, bronchials, liver, adrenals, heart, brain, arteries—and undoubtedly the toes as well!

Nutritionists have known for years that smoking depletes vitamins and minerals from the body, and that it adds harmful materials that the body must deal with. Dr. E. Cheraskin, M.D., D.M.S., points out that "nicotine disturbs the digestive system by impairing vitamin C absorption and interferes with blood circulation. By constricting the blood vessels, nicotine robs the brain of its supply of essential nutrients. Nicotine encourages hypoglycemia by causing an increased release of adrenal hormones. These raise the level of glucose in the blood, stimulating a further release of insulin—and the hypoglycemic cycle is once again underway."

There are thousands of other clinical studies on the devastating effects of smoking on the body. Most importantly, the polynuclear hydrocarbons, or tars, from smoke are known to cause mutations in the DNA blueprint in cells, resulting in birth defects and cancer, the fermenting activity in an anaerobic environment. Also, acetaldehydes, contained in smoke, cause molecules, such as amino acids and nucleic acids, to form strange alliances or molecular bonds, that harden tissue and cause abnormal environments. Heavy metals in smoke, such as lead, cadmium, polonium, and arsenic, interfere with normal enzyme function, therefore restricting virtually every chemical reaction in the body. In fact, for practically every nutrient known there has been a study conducted, showing that tobacco use interferes with the nutrient's function.

Clearly, a complete list of nutrients that smoking interferes with would probably run the entire list of known nutrients. On the other side of the coin, there are some nutrients that help offset the effects of smoking, such as vitamins A, B complex, C, D, E, selenium, zinc, and the amino acid cysteine.

If smoking is really so harmful, why are people not more aware of it? Why do smokers not get sick right away, so that the message becomes obvious? The fact that it takes several years for the smoking damage to become apparent allows smokers to rationalize that smoking really is not hurting them, that they are really getting away with it. Few people want to admit that they are wishing a slow death on themselves, and even worse, a lower quality of life before death. Remember that each cigarette helps smokers feel better while it is killing them.

And many advertisements support such thinking. In the summer of 1988, here in Austin, billboards went up showing a camel and the words "75 years and still smokin'. Camel Cigarettes." In addition to conveying the notice that the cigarette company is already 75 years in business, the billboard also contains a subliminal message that people can get away with smoking, that they can smoke for 75 years and still be able to smoke and be a part of a tradition. Such thoughts reinforce the notion that cancer only happens to the other smoker.

To fully understand the answer to the question how people get away with smoking, we must have some awe and respect for the human body, and some humility regarding its incredible functioning. The answer is this: the human body was originally designed to function in perfect health. Therefore, it has systems beyond comprehension for regulating the continuation of life. Many health authorities believe that persons following the basic laws of health, such as peaceful attitudes, proper exercise, avoidance of detrimental chemical, and proper diet, can live up to 144 years in good health. That is the body's minimum potential.

The body also has an elaborate system of compensations as well as an inherent order of sacrificing body tissue during stress. These characteristics make up the homeostasis of the entire system. Smokers' bodies have established a homeostasis that functions in the presence of tobacco poisons. With this additional stress the body cannot possibly function as well as it could, if it were free from these poisons. But the body is so resilient and well designed that it does a noble job for the smoker, in the face of unbelievable hardships.

The case for improving nutrition is universally accepted. Few persons will deny it. Many people are well aware that Americans are overfed and undernourished. In the midst of plenty we poison our bodies with expensive, addictive substances. If consideration is given to the depleted condition of America's farmland, the lack of fresh foods, the toxic conditions of the air, and water we use, it is not hard to prove the case for a little nutritional supplementation. Notice the word "little," because supplements cannot replace a wholesome diet.

Smokers, and alcohol and coffee drinkers as well, require even more nutritional support than the average person. This is obvious, because a life-style that relies on these substances is burning the candle at both ends.

Many people have the idea regarding their use of detrimental substances that they can break even by taking supplements. But that is simply not possible. A continuously harmful habit cannot be compensated for by taking health supplements. If anyone claims that this is possible, they are trying to sell you something. For one thing, smoking inhibits cellular function or the cells' ability to accept nutrients, therefore it is harder for a smoker to reap true benefit from diet or supplements. A smoker who takes the proper supplements can certainly reduce the impact and delay the effects of the smoke's toxic substances, but the compensation will not equal the damage. If anything, the stress of smoking, and then neutralizing it again and again, would cause excessive wear and tear on the body's systems.

Concerning the supplements, the word "proper" is emphasized, because so many of them on the market today are there for only one purpose—to make money for someone. Such supplements are not on the market, despite their claims, to help people be healthy. Actually, many nutritional supplements are full of inorganic or synthetic substances in addition to low quality ingredients. In fact, many of these products are sold as "natural" vitamins. Proper supplementation must be founded on bioenergy, not on milligrams and exotic ingredients. Our total health cannot be put into a test tube. Computers cannot figure out what nutrition everyone needs. Instead, health is an individual matter based on a person's metabolic rate, mineral reserves, enzyme pattern, liver activity, mental state, and individual bioenergy pattern.

Millions of dollars are spent each year on useless, excessive, and poor quality supplements. Not only does supplementation with poorly made products not get the job done, in many cases such products are detrimental to the person's health. Why? There are many answers! Because people take acidifying minerals, when their bodies are already too acid. They take vitamins that further activate the already exhausted adrenals. People use soy protein powders in fruit juice and flood their bodies with undigestible, large molecule amino acid chains. Then they wonder why they are afflicted with allergies. Poor quality products are particularly the case with sales people involved with high-powered, multi-level marketing companies. The louder and more emotional the sales pitch is, for example, with video shows, rallies, testimonials and big name athletic endorsements, the lower the quality and less beneficial the products usually are, in effect. The bigger the hype, the poorer the product. The company's money has to be spent somewhere, and in this country the money often goes into marketing, not health!

There are a few companies which base their products on genuine nutritional insight and research. These are most often small labs that have a strong dedication to healing through nutrition. People who find their way to such companies are indeed fortunate, because they have the opportunity to experience what real nutrition can do to heal and rebuild the body.

A. Stuart Wheelwright, for example, devoted much of his life to the study of nutritional energy. He cautioned people against taking individual vitamins, minerals, and amino acids (unless recommended by a competent health professional), because such substances lack the synergism, or balance, and completeness of nature. No vitamin is found alone in nature. Instead, vitamins are always in the presence of synergists, other nutrients that have a profound effect on the safety and proper use of a vitamin. Individual, isolated vitamins become chemicals rather than nutrients.

Wheelwright cautioned people against taking high-potency and complex vitamin-mineral supplements, because science cannot take all the individual ingredients and put them back together in a pill in a way that the body recognizes them. Clinical tests show that most of the vitamin formulas available today will be okay for a few people, not offer much to a lot of people, and actually be detrimental to a few people as well.

Wheelwright also advised people to supplement their diets with low-potency, honestly natural vitamins that have been chelated with herbal enzymators and minerals based on sea water which, in turn, is also chelated with sea vegetation. Wheelwright pioneered the work of nutritional synergism: that certain nutrients must work together with other nutrients. He revolutionized the nutrition industry with his research on herbal chelators which allow supplements to be made that will enhance the body energies for most people. He has developed the kind of supplements that work to support the body's life energies. For information on his nutritional breakthroughs, you can request information from a health professional working with the innovative Systemic Concept.

The basic message here is not to begin indiscriminate vitamin or mineral taking. Rather, consultation with a competent nutritionist or doctor, one who understands energy-based nutrition, is the best approach.

NUTRITIONAL PROGRAMS FOR PEOPLE QUITTING SMOKING

The following nutritional programs are based on clinical research, and have been designed to provide people nutritional support to help the stop-smoking process. Formulas referred to are those designed by A. Stuart Wheelwright. Your health professional can further tailor such a program to your individual needs, as well as answer questions. These programs have proven themselves effective time after time.

Phase one is to stop the addictive activity, supply energy supports, help with withdrawal symptoms, detoxify the body of addicting chemicals, and assist pH. This helps to break the addiction.

Phase two is to support the lung's rebuilding process. The following is an example of such nutritional support.

Basic Energy Support (Example):

AZV (A to Z vitamins)	1 each with 1 meal per day
MIN (Multi-enzymated mineral)	2 caps with 2 meals per day
CTV (Therapeutic vitamin C)	3 tabs with each meal plus 3 tabs at 4 other times per day
Ga (Adrenal)	2 caps, 3 times a day, without food
Nc (Calm)	1 cap with each Ga and 2 at bedtime
BSV (B-complex)	1 capsule with 2 meals a day

For a more comprehensive support program add:

LEV (Liquid lecithin)	3 caps with each meal
CAL (7-source calcium)	2 tabs with 2 meals
Amino acids which support neurotransmitters	

Continue this program for one month after you quit smoking. Then, usually the Nc formula can be deleted, and the CTV reduced to 2 tabs 3 times a day. Reduce Ga (Adrenal) to 2 capsules, 2 times a day, and continue for another month.

If your practitioner uses homeopathy, remedies such as Nux Vomica, Daphna Indicus, Valeriana, Veratrum Alb., Ignatia, Coffea, Moschus, Tobaccum, Passiflora, Humulus, or the Bach Flower Remedies, such as Agrimony, Rescue, and Crab Apple are effective. Enzymatic therapy may be recommended to assist the pH to alkalize.

Adjunct supplements which may be referred by your nutritionist may include Gf (Thyroid), Gb (Pituitary), ACP or ACX (Vitamin Detox), and GOLD (Immune Plus) depending on your individual needs. All supplements are foods for dietary use only. No claims are made about the supplements as they are simply foods for dietary use. GOLD is a particularly important adjunct to successfully stopping smoking. It seems to help break the addiction impulse, and to reduce the severity of the urges during withdrawal. Use 1 cap 4 times a day, particularly when urges occur. Note that GOLD may cause a niacin flush.

OTHER PROGRAMS. Following the Basic Energy Support Program, the Liver Triad Program is recommended to assist the basic, biochemical healing processes. Reading the book, *The Liver Triad* (Tips, 1989), leads to understanding why the liver program is such a vital part of your nutritional well-being. This program helps clean out stored-up residues from smoking and thus makes the clean break from the cumulative effects of smoking.

Following this program, the Lung Rebuilding Program (2 R [Lung] twice a day, 2 DCSU three times a day) is designed to strengthen and renew the respiratory system. Practitioners experienced in systemic herbology most often include the biocommand formulas #5 (Stabilizer) followed by #6 (Healer) in conjunction with the R (Lung) formula to enhance the healing resoponse. See your nutritionist or health professional for these simple, effective, and completely safe nutritional programs.

The body can recover from the effects of smoking. A person can re-eam health by working with the basic designs of the body. This material has been presented for educational purposes.

WEIGHT GAIN: THE BANE OF QUITTING

Some people prefer to smoke rather than fight to switch. And the battle of the bulge is commonly a fight that may be related to the altered brain chemistry of tobacco users as well as to a hypoglycemic (low blood sugar) pattern.

The preceding discussion has shown how nicotine acts as a stimulus barrier. And once the nicotine supply line is cut by stopping smoking, there is a need to reestablish this barrier function with natural substances. This means that the body requires nutrition that can support the acetylcholine production in the brain.

However, there are other brain chemicals that might help in a pinch, one is seratonin which is involved in the sleep process. Serotonin, like nicotine, is a vasoconstrictor, meaning that it tightens blood vessels and raises blood pressure. In the brain, serotonin has a sedative effect which is something of a stimulus barrier.

Perhaps this is why people who quit smoking often crave carbohydrates, such as bread, potatoes, snack foods, and cereals. Carbohydrates, when eaten without vegetables to buffer them, cause a release of serotonin in the brain and thus are considered sedatives. This sedative effect is a concern regarding the diet programs which are built on complex carbohydrates. On such diets people often loose their energy. An optimal eating plan is described in the book, *Pro-Vita! Diet* (Tips, 1989).

There are other causes of weight gain. Both smoking and eating are used as a conscious or subconscious signal to indicate completion of a task, or to delay starting a task. People involved in this reward, or procrastination, relationship with eating and smoking may be inclined to eat more when they cut off one of the options, like smoking.

Also, smoking interferes with the communication among master glands, the hypothalamus, pituitary, and adrenals. One function of this part of the complex of body systems is appetite regulation. Therefore, it is no wonder that appetite can be an issue when smoking is stopped.

Without the stimulation of tobacco, the body's metabolic rate can drop even lower, causing weight gain due to storage of fats. For this reason, some health professionals recommend metabolic support (Gf + #1), when weight gain is occurring. Nutritionists can recommend herbal supplements, or beverages, containing the Chinese herb ma-huang or the American herb, Mormon Tea, both of which contain ephedra, to speed up the metabolism and decrease the appetite.

By relying on nutrition with herbs, supplements, and living foods to help in the transition, people do not have to eat their way out of addictions at the expense of their health. Obesity is a health hazard, and there is not much sense in substituting one hazard for another. As with so many areas of health, nutrition and natural therapies offer the best way to restore the vitality people want.

STOPPING SMOKING IS STRESSFUL: NUTRITION CAN HELP

As more is learned about the body's chemistry, metabolic processes, and energies, the more obvious it is how critical the role of proper nutrition becomes. And nutrition is particularly important in helping people with the stress of withdrawal from the current addictive state into one of more optimal health. This fact is better documented every year.

For years, great nutritionists have taught us that life-giving foods provide the vital ingredients for our health, longevity, and freedom from disease. With the wonderful technologies of medical research, the role of nutrition can now be proven. A great debt is owed to doctors and researchers who have dared to investigate nutrition as a healing science.

To properly apply nutrition, such as food and supplements, the nutritional counselor must understand both the metabolic role of foods, and what is involved in changing a person's metabolic state. The use of tobacco exercises a strong influence upon the body's chemical balance and energy systems. Therefore, abruptly stopping this influence means that the body must adjust to a new metabolic process. Such change, in turn, means stress.

When people have a deep commitment to stop smoking, they are experiencing a resurgence of their life force, their innate drive for a full, healthful life. This is a beautiful thing to behold, because it is an opportunity to be reborn. Such a rebirth is represented by the desire and commitment to break away from tobacco.

People who seek ways to stop smoking are expressing their affirmation of life, a revolution against a tyrant that can only deal them unhappiness and death. But people must understand how best to pull themselves out of the smoking habit. Nothing is more discouraging than people who try and fail, because each failure is a symbol of subservience to powers that appear to be greater than the human spirit. It is heartbreaking to see people suffer under such an addiction illusion because this illusion has such a strong bearing on their quality of life and happiness, and that of others as well.

For this very reason it is important to get the odds in your favor when you begin an effort to quit smoking. Eliminate potential stumbling blocks. Guarantee your success from day one. Say out loud to yourself: "Not smoking is simple. I just put it away and out of my life. I am free from smoking. I choose life." Then begin your program of retraining your mind/body patterns, stress management, and nutritional support.

NOW YOU CAN QUIT SMOKING: DESIGN A PLAN

Now, more than ever before, you are able to quit smoking, quit forever, and become totally free so that tobacco has no allure for you. To do this, you need a plan. A good way to develop a plan is to take a pencil and paper and design one.

Phase One of your plan is to write down all of the good things, all of the benefits, all the positive aspects that stopping smoking can bring. Title this exercise "The Joys of Independence from Tobacco" and make a list of everything terrific you can expect in your life when you are no longer involved with smoking.

Here are a few pointers from a previous class to stimulate your own thoughts. If you absolutely agree with one item written here, you must write it down on your own list and make it yours!

- I'll save $1000 a year by not buying cigarettes,
  by getting a lower rate on my homeowner's insurance,
  by getting a lower rate on my health insurance.
- I'll:
  - plan a vacation,
  - use the savings to pursue nutritional counsel for
    improving my health,
  - build an addition to the house,
  - invest it for retirement.
- I'll be able to make more friends. I've found that I missed opportunities to date someone because I smoke.
- I'll stop my current progress toward cancer.
  I will reverse the trend and be truly healthy.
- My breath won't stink anymore and my smile will be brighter.
- I'll be a better role model for my children, and be an example on how to overcome adversity.
- By affirming life rather than committing slow suicide, I'll create a new life for myself in all areas.
- I'll save money on dry cleaning.
- I'll get rid of my chronic, hacking cough.
- For my children's health, our home environment will be smoke free.

And there are many more reasons. The above examples came from the first class's worksheets and were the items that they were willing to share.

After writing down all of your reasons, lay your list aside and give it a day or two to incubate. Then review your list, add to it, and polish the language to get it exactly right.

At this point, in the planning stages, it is important to pick a date on which you will stop smoking. As most people know, there are basically two ways to stop—cold turkey, and gradually cutting down. Different types of people do best with one technique or the other.

The book, *Conquer Candida* (Tips, 1989), contains a discussion of the constitutional types of human beings according to Wheelwright, the "turkey", the "chicken", and the "lurkey". Turkeys are robust, active, coarse-mannered people; chickens are delicate, passive, and fine-mannered people; lurkeys are somewhere in the middle with characteristics of both the turkey and chicken.

The turkey type of person can quit smoking "cold turkey," a slang phrase that means to quit an addiction abruptly, all at once. These are the people who crumple up the pack of cigarettes and stop!

The chicken type of person is best accommodated by cutting back gradually a week before stopping completely. These people switch to milder cigarettes, gradually cut back on the number per day, and then stop completely. This method gives their systems less of a shock, or rather it stretches out the duration of agitation so it is handled little by little rather than all at once.

The lurkey people must decide for themselves which way to quit. Perhaps a quick cut-back and then stopping is a good way for them. If the person prefers to dive into cold water and get it over with, then the cold turkey approach might be the best. If the person gets into cold water an inch at a time, prolonging the pain, taking it gradually, then the cut-back-before-quitting approach may suit them better.

Regardless of the technique, choose a date on which you absolutely will quit. Mark it on your calendar. And live by it!

The next preliminary step is to begin your basic nutritional support. As we have learned earlier in this chapter, there are many supplemental supports. What you choose depends on the areas you most need to support. Here are some areas for consideration:

- Basic nutrition: moderate potency multi vitamin, multi mineral formula. (High potency formulas can cause additional stress.)

- Vitamin C: to help flush out the residual poisons.
- Niacin: to reduce withdrawal symptoms.
- Amino acids and synergists to support the brain's neurotransmitters as follows (all in one formula):
  - DL-phenylalanine: to inhibit enkaphalinase,
  - L-phenylalanine: to increase catecholalmine levels,
  - L-glutamine: to increase GABA to suppress firing of dopaminergic neurons, preventing over-stimulation,
  - Pyridoxal-5-phosphate: a co-factor to produce brain amines, enhances intestinal absorption.
  - Note: L-tryptophan can increase serotonin levels and be of benefit, but the FDA has ruled that it is dangerous due to contamination by a Japanese lab and it is no longer included in amino acid formulas at this time.
- Nutrients: Lecithin, Choline, Inositol.
- Glandular support: Adrenal, Thyroid, Hypothalamus.
- Nerve support: soothing, calming formulas.
- Homeopathic support: individually designed remedies to assist detox of tobacco by-products and stimulate adjustment to natural health.
- Liver detox support: herbs to cleanse residues of tars and tobacco chemicals.

The nutritional support can greatly assist with withdrawal and help lessen the pain of transition. Nutritional support can help the habit-breaking process to occur quicker. It can also make the transition more thorough, increase the opportunity for complete recovery so that reoccurrence does not happen, and help the body rebuild and establish a new homeostasis—one that is free from addiction.

Some people cannot financially afford to do a comprehensive nutritional support program, though the benefits are well worth the cost, so I am often asked what is the bare minimum that a person can get by with.

My reply is the following: 1) eat salads and lightly steamed vegetables with each meal (including breakfast). See the *Pro-Vita! Diet* for optimal nutrition. Eating well increases the person's overall nutritional values. 2) Use the Ga (Adrenal), and Nc (Calm) herbal formulas to support the biological energy processes. 3) Use a homeopathic remedy to support the bioenergetic processes. 4) Use a brain formula to assist the addiction-transition process.

Anything added to that basic plan can help, but the basic plan covers what most people require to be successful.

At this point you have a list of benefits and a quitting plan with a date. Obtain the nutritional supplements and any other support you choose such as acupuncture, massage, an exercise regimen, colonic irrigations, lemonade diet (fast), for example.

Some people have had success with hypnotism, but I do not recommend it. The implanted suggestion does not reach the core issues, and the addiction is not broken. Instead, it is only put on the back burner for a while. With hypnotism, the patient is not the winner, the suggestion is. The patient does not process the problem into victory and learn from it. Hypnotism is a trick or an artificial implant which achieves a result, but not a complete solution.

Many people find that it is helpful to tell other persons that they are quitting smoking and the date on which they are absolutely quitting. This can be supportive if the people are chosen with discrimination. They can offer encouragement and support.

If you like the idea of telling others, be sure to tell those that will support you from the heart. Be certain that those whom you tell about your plan have no vested interest in your continuing to smoke, such as a friend who has been unable to quit and does not want to admit that you are the stronger person should you succeed.

Now, with the odds in your favor, you can quit, make the transition, and rebuild your health. You can be successful and end the tobacco habit once and for all. Just do it!

The next step for you to take is support via attitudinal adjustments. This topic has a chapter to itself.

11 _____

GREATER ENERGY:
THE NUTRITIONAL SOLUTION

KEEP A LIGHT PERSPECTIVE

Just to keep our perspective, this book is not intended to be another anti-fun nutrition text. The good life does not really begin until a person has a stable degree of health. And fun certainly is not dependent on health-destroying activities. When you feel terrific, having fun will be all the more enjoyable!

The experienced nutritionist can see both sides of an issue. Copper deficient people can use a little chocolate until they normalize their mineral levels. Slow oxidizers (people who are metabolically slow in converting nutrients to energy) may benefit from a little wine which perks up the metabolic rate. The point here is that addictive substances cause nutritional and energy deficits (both emotional and Kreb's cycle physical energy) and lead a person to chronic and degenerative diseases. In the instance where people have a biochemic susceptibility or genetic proclivity to alcohol dependence, alcohol must be completely avoided.

In the book, *The Pro-Vita! Diet* (Tips, 1989), the following message is contained: "It's not what you do ten percent of the time, it's what you do ninety percent of the time that sets the standards for your health." This is true for the majority of people, although there are a few exceptions, such as people susceptible to alcohol. Of course, vibrant energy is the bottom line in health. A person with stable energy levels can enjoy an occasional food item on the hit list without great harm. The key, again, seems to be moderation and an understanding and practice of balance in your life.

It is important to realize that the healthy body has no innate desires for alcohol, tobacco, sugar, marijuana, mood altering drugs, coffee, or excessive activities. It is not a matter of suffering through life without any "fun" items. The healthy body simply does not define fun as having anything to do with artificial stimulants.

You are free of an addiction or addictive tendency when you can pass by the substance and not even notice it. The dessert cart is just another menu item, not even very interesting. The cigarette machines and soda vending machines are just bulky boxes getting in the way of foot traffic. The formerly addictive item no longer has any pull and you view it dispassionately as an object. As long as a person wishes he or she could sample the dessert cart, as long as the vending machines trigger a response or brief regret that "I really can't, but I wish I could", then the person is still actively involved in the energy addiction.

Will power may be keeping the person on the straight and narrow, but the person is not yet free or happy. But through the Systemic Plan, the goal is to be completely free of any attachment to the formerly substance. This occurs when the body is biochemically and bioenergetically balanced. And such a state means more than just avoiding cancer by stopping smoking. Instead, it means all the good and fun things in life such as joy, energy, patience, healthy libido, good health, clear thinking, healthy skin, sparkle in the eyes, spring in the step, and freedom from disease.

ADDICTIONS AND NUTRITIONAL DEFICIENCIES

We know that addictions and addictive tendencies are based on glandular/hormonal energy deficiencies, closely aligned with faulty meridian bioenergy or biochemical energy (endorphins, enkephalins, vitamins, minerals, amino acids). These conditions are founded in most cases of nutritional deficiencies. Which came first, the energy deficiency or the addictive tendency, varies from person to person. This does not really matter here because nutrition plays a constructive role in either case.

Consequently, we can understand that the use of stimulants and addictive activities is not so much an immoral act, as some people have claimed, but instead represents the demand by the body for pseudo energy in a "make-do" situation which is due to a chemical or energy imbalance. Of course, for some people addictions are a way of escaping the pain of living, or of improving how they feel as stress takes its toll. But this condition, too, is based on a nutritional issue. Both the pain of living and the effects of emotional stress can be improved via nutrition.

Any stress on the body can be handled better and processed by a balanced, healthy, nutrient-rich body. This does not mean, for example, that the passing of a loved one is not going to cause grief. But the body's ability to deal with and process the grief, and recover is largely based on the avoidance of artificial pain killers, such as drugs and alcohol.

Addictive activities rob the body of nutrients and bioenergy and thus create the need for repetition of the addiction. Think about each addictive activity we have discussed. Compulsive activity burns nutrients at an alarming rate. Water soluble vitamins and trace minerals are washed out of the body during the stress of hyper-activity. Sugar is known to deplete a host of important vitamins and minerals. Coffee, tea, and sodas do likewise. Certainly we know that tobacco and marijuana deplete nutrients and require higher levels of Vitamin C just to repair the damage. Loud noises take a nutritional toll also. When the volume is cranked way up on the stereo or headphones, rock 'n' roll as well as other kinds of music can cause a stress response. Compulsive jogging (note: compulsive does not include a regular fitness program for healthy people) breaks down muscles, spends amino acids and minerals, which are difficult to replace in a nutrient depleted body. (And, Gatorade simply does not replace the nutrients required to rebuild healthy tissue.) Excessive use of salt causes mineral imbalances and loss through the urine. Excessive ejaculation removes a rich supply of nutrients (zinc, amino acids) from the body. And lastly, alcohol and drugs (recreational and prescription) deplete a host of nutrients.

Thus, the pervasive theme of addictive activities is that a person expends nutrients when participating in such behaviors.

We want to thoroughly break the illusion that a cup of coffee, or a cigarette, or a candy bar gives you something. These addictive substances are like the loan shark that gives money, but the interest rate makes it nearly impossible to repay the debt.

It is interesting to note the difference between recreational drug use in the 1960s and the late 1980s. In the '60s, it was linked with idealism, rebellion, self-exploration as well as hopes for mind expansion and spiritual growth. But the promise of drugs proved to be a destructive illusion. In the '80s, drug use has degenerated into an admission of the inability to make life work. And all that is available from drug use now is detrimental escape, hedonistic highs, poor attempts to cope with stress, and temporary oblivion. In effect, drug use further separates users from their connection with life, the very connection that brings joy and spiritual adventures. To cope with the stress of life, people must find non-destructive ways that allow them growth and fulfillment.

Escape provides no answers. Only confrontation with the issues of life can resolve the inner need for escape, after which a reconnecting with the life force can revitalize a person by bringing life, activity, enjoyment, and adventure back into the person's orbit.

We can also see that prescriptions for corrective drugs, like ritalin, norpremin, darvon, lithium, for example, most often only palliate the symptoms. These drugs rarely affect the cause of illness or disease, which we now know to be an imbalance in the energy systems on the nutritional, hormonal, meridian, and chemical levels. These energy levels constitute body systems that respond well to nutrition. Inorganic drugs do not cure, instead they only fix or suppress symptoms. Most drugs are not compatible with the body's life systems, although they do cause precise reactions in living organisms. And there is a place for them. Lithium, for example, has certainly saved manic-depressives' lives. It has not cured them, however.

Medicine, as well as natural therapies, cannot cure, only the body itself can. Generally speaking, drugs are so effective

173

at suppressing symptoms that they often block the body's ability to heal itself. On the other hand, drugs can be so traumatic that they foster a healing response by providing enough trauma to evoke a healing reaction. But a two-by-four applied to the rear end might evoke the same healing response. Most drugs are non-living. Even plant-derrived drugs, once isolated, standardized and processed contain little remembrance of their biological sources. In contrast, herbs, natural supplements, and homeopathics resonate with life-compatible energy.

Fifty years ago, people often died at an early age of infectious diseases, such as tuberculosis, pneumonia, scarlet fever, and syphilis. Now, largely due to wonder drugs, vaccines, and antibiotics, infectious diseases are not so threatening. In exchange, we have become a people afflicted with chronic degenerative diseases, caused in part by wonder drugs as well as by poor diet, and the overall philosophy that we can indulge in destructive behavior, because medical science can fix whatever ails us. The current pandemic of candida albicans infections is an example of how antibiotics have caused widespread degenerative diseases in people. For further information on this see the book, *Conquer Candida* (Tips, 1989).

The longer life span provided by applications of drug medicine ends up being spent in and out of hospitals, fighting degenerative diseases like arthritis, osteoporosis, cancer or diabetes; losing various body parts to surgery; blasting various parts with radioactive materials or poisoning the system with deadly chemotherapies. Some people question the value of long, but poor quality, life spans. But nutrition, on the other hand, builds and supports the basic and regenerative life systems of the body, while concurrently providing protection from the stress of life as well. The promise of nutrition is a healthy, active elder life.

An ever growing number of people want to work with herbs, nutrition, and homeopathics first, to seek the help of drugs only as a last resort. The famous medical doctor, Francisco Xavier Eizayaga of Buenos Aires, Argentina, has effected cures of leukemia, lupus, cancer, multiple sclerosis, asthma, dementia, as well as the infectious diseases such as gonorrhea, pneumonia, syphilus, nephritis, meningitis without ever resorting to drugs. His successes as a clinician rival anyone's in the entire world. When asked how often he had to abandon homeopathic treatment and instead use drugs to save a person, he replied: "I have never used a drug."

The general nutritional advice for people involved with addictive substances—about 95% of us—is to return to the fundamentals of nutrition. The first step is to increase the consumption of alkalizing foods which means eating more vegetables, both raw and lightly steamed. Occasionally, people are too alkaline. But the general trend today is that people are too acid due to adrenal burnout and overconsumption of acid-forming foods, such as red meat, dairy products, and sodas. Stress causes an over-acid con-dition, also.

While briefly mentioning pH information, it is worthwhile to note that there is a state of acidness, or acid pH, that rep-resents in reality a very deep alkalosis, in which the body has locked into a pH of 5 for self-protection. A test of the urine or saliva pH with special litmus paper can help determine the pH state. Ask your nutritionist for pHydrion low-buff pH paper, or to conduct a 24-hour urinalysis.

Of the basic food groups, fruits and vegetables are the most alkalizing. The other foods, meat, dairy and grains, are primarily acid-forming. However, many grains are fairly neutral and not too acid-forming to the urine. Acids stimulate the energy glands, and make the body work to neutralize them by using sodium and calcium, which are alkaline minerals. Since vegetables and fruits contain good amounts of these alkalizing minerals, one of the best things a person can do therefore is to eat more vegetables, and fruit if candida is not a problem. This advice is based on the assumption that most people are currently eating the Standard American Diet (SAD) of meat, fried potatoes, sweets, and fast food which represents an acid-forming, nutrient-depleted, poorly combined, high stress, high fat, low fiber, chemical-preserved, and over-cooked substance, commonly called "food".

Also, the dietary supplements, such as Green Magma, Barley Green, Greenlife, blue green algae, and chlorella, along with fresh vegetable juice, can help add the much-needed chlorophyll and vegetable-based minerals to the diet.

NUTRITIONAL SUPPORT FOR BREAKING ADDICTIONS

During the past five years several unique breakthroughs in herbology have resulted in effective nutritional programs for breaking addictions. This happened largely through the research of A.S. Wheelwright, a master herbal formulator, who combined herbs, homeopathic elements, vitamins, minerals, enzymes, DNA and RNA, protomorphagens, and free-form amino acids into bioenergetic formulas that resonate with the same patterns as the designated body system. The resulting formulas prove to be effective and comprehensive support for breaking the addictive energy cycle.

There are now available safe and effective nutritional supports to help the body change from an addictive energy system back to the body's natural energy system, including support for:

1. Weakened energy glands (thyroid, adrenal),
2. Brain glands (pituitary, hypothalamus),
3. Nerves (to soothe and strengthen),
4. Neurotransmitters (to balance endorphins and enkephalins),
5. Defeating the urge to repeat the habit,
6. Coping with the withdrawal symptoms,
7. Detoxifying poisons from the system,
8. Rebuilding damaged organs and tissue.

Natural programs to support the above have been developed at the Systemic Clinic. These programs are freely available to doctors and practicing health professionals so that they, too, can help people break their addictive patterns and experience greater health.

However, the primary ingredient in changing a self-destructive activity to something more positive, healthy, and natural is not the vitamin or herbal supplements, but the desire to change. This wish represents more than mere will power, and much more than the inspiration derived from fear upon realizing where use of the addictive substances may lead. It is a reaffirmation of life, and the inner knowledge that a life free of addictions is one of spiritual freedom, abundance, and wholeness.

Watch for the signs of addiction: activities that provide energy, and then leave you with less energy than before; activities that cause withdrawal symptoms, if you must do without them.

It must be affirmed by those of us who have let go of the many addictions, so readily supplied by our supermarkets, that the body in its inherent wisdom provides an excellent and vibrant energy to those who practice the simple rules of sound nutrition and other holistic principles, such as rest, proper structure, exercise, communication, and being of service. This natural energy is far more exciting and fulfilling than all artificial energy sources combined. Proper nutrition gives the body "spark" as well as the freedom to enjoy an occasional amaretto chocolate cheese cake—if that is what you like—without all the mental warfare. A strong nutritional foundation is fundamentally important. It must be the basis upon which to build health.

It is with much regret that I hear of alcohol cessation programs, stop smoking programs, and cocaine addiction breaking programs that do not incorporate basic nutrition as a fundamental part of the program. I know that although such programs have successes and help people, the patients and clients suffer more than they have to, or were given mood altering drugs to help with the unnecessary level of suffering from withdrawal. These programs ignore the fact that nutrition provides the brain chemicals to stabilize and normalize the addictive process; that nutrition provides the bioenergy for the body to make repairs and adjustments to its energy systems; that nutrition provides the building blocks for healing and repair. Ultimately, nutrition helps with the transition of breaking addictions, no matter what level or how severe the addictions are.

12

TRANSFORMATION: THE DOOR TO FREEDOM

AFFIRMING

Few people realize that imagination is much more powerful than will power, because imagination is a function of the heart center, while will power is a function of the brain. If people visualize clean teeth, sparkling fresh breath, healthy pink lungs, beautiful effervescent oxygen energizing the brain, and see themselves in the vibrancy of being free of addictions, and then DO something about their condition, they will harness the very power that shapes their lives.

Once the imaginative, or imaging, faculty is tapped, the new image will press forward into manifestation provided certain natural laws are observed. This will help to displace the addiction, provided that the image is genuine, and that the new image is stronger than the resistance against it.

When people can truly establish a self-image that is not addicted, the addiction will drop away. Saying "I am a smoker," or "I am an alcoholic," can be self-defeating. This certainly may be a step better than pretending that the addictions do not exist, because this is a step toward self-honesty and self-responsibility; but who wants to reinforce negative images! Therefore, it would be much better to say: "I used to be an alcoholic, but now I am no longer, because I am free." This image reinforces the dropping away of the alcoholic tendency. I used to be an ignorant child, but I don't go around telling this everybody everyday.

Human beings can be free of their diseases. People can be free of their addictions. They do not have to wear them like badges at a convention!

See yourself free, affirm yourself free, imagine yourself free, contemplate what life is like exactly as you want it to be—and then be free. Go beyond acknowledging the addiction into the realization that the addiction is of no concern whatsoever. Such realization represents a neutral state of being neither for nor against the addiction. It means that you are no longer attached to your addiction or attached to fighting your addiction; both of which represent a hold on your freedom.

It is amazing how fast addictions can drop away with a comprehensive approach of:

- nutrition/homeopathy,
- visualization or use of the imaging faculty,
- manifestation via action.

HOMEOPATHY:
HARNESS YOUR VITAL FORCE

Homeopathy, along with the sciences of acupuncture and systemic herbology, is a premier healing science that is concerned with cure, rather than amelioration of symptoms. It is a system of medicine that is preoccupied with correcting the cause of symptoms instead of manipulating the body to pretend it doesn't have symptoms.

If you are not familiar with homeopathy as a healing science, please read the appendix to *The Pro-Vita! Plan for Optimal Nutrition* (Tips, 1992). Homeopathy has been suppressed in the United States, but is a widely practiced, highly respected system of medicine throughout the world.

Symptoms are simply the body's Vital Force expressing its struggle to maintain health, or it's most optimal balance of function, despite all the forces that make it difficult -- poor diet, poor attitude, environmental challenges, constitutional predispositions to illness, and so forth. Thus symptoms serve as a guide to where the body is struggling to maintain homeostasis or it's most optimal balance.

The Vital Force is your body's instinctive healing mechanism that is dedicated to maintaining an environment for life to flourish. It calls upon your body's innate resources to adapt to whatever the environment demands so your life is preserved in the most optimal condition it is able to maintain. The Vital Force is the body's healing mechanism. It operates according to the Natural Laws known only to those who study the natural cure of the body. Thus it is virtually unknown to those who practice medicine as it is taught in the western world, but it is well known to those who practice homeopathy, acupuncture, and systemic herbology.

179

In the case of addictions, the body has learned to adapt to the presence of the addictive substance or activity, and the addiction has become a part of the homeostatic operation. But, since the addiction causes less than optimal symptoms, there is a clear basis for selecting a constitutional homeopathic remedy that can help stimulate the Vital Force to make a correction toward cure and a more optimal level of health.

In clinical practice, clients often report, "I've been on this blood pressure for four years now. It helps me maintain a more normal blood pressure."

My reply is, "Four years? When it is going to cure you so you don't need the drug anymore?" After all, isn't the mission of the physician to restore health?

This is an example of Medicine's failure to correct the cause of the problem. Medicine knows how to manipulate the body to pretend it doesn't have the symptom, but it doesn't know how to cure. When this occurs, the fundamental imbalance or disease is left intact with the likelihood it will become a deeper pathology.

The homeopathic approach simply asks the body to rise to a more optimal state of function, based on the fact that a more optimal level is inherent.

But the body can cure itself with the right information so the Vital Force is stimulated to make a complete correction of the cause, provided it is possible. In the case of high blood pressure, the body chooses or allows that symptom to manifest because it is the best way to cope or adapt to a set of circumstances that it is unable to completely manage with the resources it has available.

Perhaps the kidneys are weak. Perhaps the circulation to the brain is weak. Perhaps there is constriction in the arterial passages. Thus, the rise in blood pressure is the best temporary way to meet the body's demands for circulation to the brain or for the kidneys to filter more important materials from the blood. Whatever the cause of high blood pressure, having that symptom is the best the body can do at the time.

But the drug medication obviously does not correct the cause. It only forces the body to lower the blood pressure and still maintain its disease or less than optimal condition. This is just one reason why drug medicine has so many side effects. Some side effects come from the presence of the poisonous drug in the system. Yet other side effects come from the suppression of the symptom since this forces the Vital Force to have to cope with the inherent problem through other means, often a deeper disturbance of the body's equilibrium.

On the other hand, the homeopathic medicine stimulates the body to correct the cause -- in this case the weak kidneys or the need for circulation to the brain or to pass blood through constricted arteries. And when this is done, the body no longer needs or allows the blood pressure to be high. It regulates and balances itself.

Thus, we find in the natural therapies, a respect for the body's inherent healing processes. This is why the natural therapies must stay focused on the Laws of Natural Cure and always seek to work with the body's healing force rather than inflict an external medicine that dictates a response regardless of what the body's healing processes might be.

Now, with addictions, homeopathy helps the body draw upon its Vital Force and seek an internal correction to the situation. The homeopathic remedy reaches in very deep and draws upon the Vital Force at a level that is deeper than the addiction-process. Thus, although homeopathy is an exceedingly gentle method of stimulating the Vital Force to react, it is extremely powerful if it stimulates the Vital Force deeper than the cause of the addiction. When this occurs, the body's healing forces are focused on correcting the addictive process and harnesses its deep healing resources to do so.

When the addictive substance or activity is removed from the person, the body must seek a new level of homeostasis. This can cause a period of discomfort known as withdrawal which can also be accompanied with other cleansing symptoms as the body endeavors to establish a new metabolic system of operation. Careful observation of these symptoms, the symptoms of change, may or may not lead the homeopathic physician to recommend an acute remedy to help with the transition process

Thus, the constitutional homeopathic remedy, administered as a single dose, is a powerful ally in the natural correction of the addictive process. Such a remedy must be chosen by a competent classical homeopath as a result of the homeopathic interview process. It is usually not found by electronic means, muscle testing, or radionics evaluation. It is found by careful observation of the homeopathic practitioner applying the criteria specified in Dr. Samuel Hahnemann's *Organon of Medicine* which, briefly, include 1) Totality of Symptoms, 2) Etiology, 3) Time and Progression, 4) Miasms, 5) Temperament, 6) Constitution, and modern-day homeopaths also apply an overall consideration know as 7) Essence. When these seven considerations are applied with an understanding of the whole person, the Vital Force is able to utilize all its resources to restore the body to its most optimal level of health.

Oftentimes, accompanying the deep stimulation of the body's innate vitality with the homeopathic remedy, is a renewed self-love or more positive self image. Self esteem is a natural and fundamental component of good health. It is also the faculty that is most often disturbed by addictions because every time the addictive process is indulged in it strengthens the illusion that the addiction is stronger than the individual. Thus, we find that the homeopathic remedy can impact a person at the deepest level -- the mind.

THE NEXT STEP TO SELF MASTERY

There is an old adage: "You can't love others until you love yourself." Self-loathing causes many limitations in their lives. Learning to forgive yourself and recognize that you were doing the best you could with what you had to work with in the past, can release the inner tension that inhibits your life expression. This tension may well be the root of an addictive process that keeps you chained to the illusion of poor self-worth.

By breaking the addictive pattern, a person takes a step toward self-worth and self-mastery. This step can open the door to an entirely new life experience.

In this sense, breaking an addictive pattern is simply an example or archetype of a person's move to greater freedom. This move results in greater joy and greater experiences in life. Prior to the breakthrough the addiction held the person back in some areas of life, but not to the extent that it was readily noticed. The addiction was merely a small manifestation of the attitudes that were causing defeat, failure, and the inability to make life work as well as possible.

Letting go of the self-limiting addiction can be a prototype for breaking other detrimental attitudes and the self-resignation which are defining a less-than-optimal life experience. Winning the addiction challenge by breaking its pattern is an example that the individual can be successful in taking constructive steps toward freedom and self-growth. Success breeds success.

The struggle to get free of an addiction can expose the attitudes behind it. When the attitudes are understood and confronted, the addiction can drop away. Whereas attitudes are often invisible to the person, the addictive pattern is not. By working with what is visible, a person can discover the cause behind it. This is why recognizing the addiction process and working to break it can be a valuable self-discovery exercise and open new doors in life.

Quitting the use of caffeine, excessive sugar, tobacco, marijuana, cocaine, or alcohol can represent a great deal more than simply protecting your health by removing a substance or activity which ruins health. In effect, conquering addictions can be a process of realizing more freedom, joy, love, and success in life.

A look at the process of manifestation shows how it can help create a life free of addictions.

IMAGING

A major key to overcoming addictions is self-image, or how we see ourselves. People who see themselves as addicts, or afflicted with a disease, are prone to failure due to that limiting attitude or mental picture of themselves. They are always struggling with their image of themselves as afflicted persons. They expend a tremendous amount of energy by applying will power against their biological and bioenergetic need for an addictive substance.

Keep in mind that nutrition can relieve so much of that craving and tension. This can free a lot of energy which can be applied toward creative visualization to build a new life from the foundation up.

The concept that what we think, and the way we think it, is critically important to a person's well-being, is readily embraced by the holistic health model, because this concept demonstrates the philosophy of the whole person. In other words, "As a man thinketh in his heart, so is he." This applies to women and children as well. The heart represents the subconscious or self-image, not the brain.

Simultaneously with the acceptance of the holistic model, scientists and doctors are discovering the patterns and pathways that connect the brain with the immune system. This means that to some extent, people can THINK their way to health when that process is properly applied. Or at least the thinking process can contribute to a greater level of health. Jean Achterberg in her book, *Imagery in Healing* (1985), and

Bernie Siegel in his text, *Peace, Love & Healing* (1989) discuss the medical and healing results of imaging.

The creative imagination is the powerful faculty that can impress the subconscious with a new self-image, which then uses the mind to shape reality. FEELING and ACTION are important constituents to manifesting what the creative imagination images. Working with the creative imagination to create a new set of circumstances, a new reality, is a recreational (re-CREATION-al) activity that can shape a new lifestyle.

In this discussion we will simplify the concepts that research about positive thinking has put forth, and explain how to use this great life-shaping power to conquer addictions.

Every human being is capable of applying the creative imagination, no matter how rusty or dusty it may be. It can be used to impress the subconscious mind which is the strongest force in shaping the reality we live. However, creative imagination is an impersonal tool that can be used both for benefit or destruction. Job said, for example: "That which I fear is upon me." These words explain how the worst that Job expected sure enough manifested in his life. But through proper use of the creative imagination, the words, "that which Ifear," can be changed into saying, "that which I love." In this way the quality of life can be dramatically improved.

To use creative imagination, simply take a quiet time, relax, and imagine the way you would like to live. If you are a smoker, spend twenty minutes a day relaxed and imagining what it is like to have healthy, pink, and clean lungs. Imagine a sweet breath that fills the space around you with well-being. Imagine a lung capacity that readily contains large volumes of life-giving air, a reflection of your desire to live full volumes of life.

If you are a drinker, imagine the focused, mental clarity of living a life that is crisp, clear, engaged, and full of joy. Imagine a body that functions with great energy and vitality, and is free of pain. Imagine people's admiration of you as they sense an inner strength and peace in your presence.

Imaging is the first step to establishing a new life-style. Such an exercise is not wishful thinking. It is a focused time of re-creating reality. Your images must be sharp and clear, a result of your full attention.

While relaxed, harness the senses and FEEL what you are imagining. This puts amperage with the voltage of your images. Feel what it is like to breathe deeply without pain or coughing. Feel life crackle around you like static electricity. Feel what it is like to have a new mastery of life and the admiration of others. Feel the wind blow through your hair and caress your face as you stand on a mountain top, affirming your love of life to the world.

SEE the smiles on people's faces as they meet you. See yourself giving to others freely from your heart as you are a person free of self-limiting habits. See the money you save for building a secure future.

HEAR the compliments of people as they meet you. Hear the praise of loved ones as they admire your accomplishments.

TASTE AND SMELL the sensations of food without the taint of smoke or the numbing of alcohol. Taste the air as it enlivens you. Smell the verdant forest redolent with the odors of the never ending cycle of birth, death, and re-birth. Smell the invigorating freshness of the dew as it sparkles on the grass at the dawn of a new day.

Make your imaginings fresh and alive. Humor all of your senses to impress the creative imagination with a complete spectrum of FEELINGS, giving depth and credence to your exercise.

To this exercise of imagining and feeling add ACTION. First, see yourself living and being successful in all your activities. Then apply this action principle when the exercise is over. This means DO SOMETHING. Act as if your wish were fulfilled. Act as if you had no addiction. Such actions, performed with the attitude that you have mastery over yourself and your addictive tendencies, affirm to the brain the newly created reality. The brain will adjust its tendencies accordingly.

Walk straight and proud with your head held up, fully aware of your surroundings. Choose a nutritional beverage. Replace the ash tray with an art object.

FOCUSED IMAGES-FEELING-ACTION! This is the triad that will impress the self-image. The mind is a weak tool compared to the subconscious. The mind is merely a candle compared to the sun-burst energy of the subconscious. Work with the subconscious, and the mind will become a powerful tool and ally to implement what the subconscious holds as real.

A new self-image can affect the body's biochemistry even in the case of alcoholism, although it is true that alcoholics have a metabolic and biochemical imbalance that leads to addiction. After all, this is the reason why alcoholism is called a disease. But even this disease state can be overcome with the help of nutritional body chemistry balancing, and a redefined self-image.

The following is a report from a patient who achieved complete mastery over alcohol. This person went far beyond the state expressed as: "I have a disease and my life is altered because of it." She went beyond the CONCEPT of complete freedom to make it a REALITY in her life.

As background to her letter: the patient, a woman, was alcoholic for fourteen years. She participated in the Systemic Program, using many of the tools outlined in this book, including private psychotherapy. After five months, she went on maintenance support and was considered free of addiction by her nutritional and psychotherapeutic counselors. The provision was that she would never touch alcohol again. Her alcohol-related allergy tested to be specifically to grapes (wine, champagne, brandy, etc.) and yeast.

Dear Jack,

Even though it's been over a year since I've touched a drop of alcohol, I never really understood that I could be 100% free. Everyone told me that I'd always have an inner longing for alcohol and that a mere sip could enslave me all over again. Well, today I've had an experience I'd like to relate to you.

First, let me catch you up on what I've been doing, since I haven't had an appointment with you in quite a while. I've continued the Liver Triad and maintenance supplementation you recommended six months ago. Occasionally I've had counseling as needed. And I've been working with the manifestation techniques regarding the psychology of spirit described in the book *The Flute of God* by Paul Twitchell, which was recommended by a friend.

Well, this morning I was having a dull headache and while at the health food store I bought a homeopathic remedy from herbs for headache. Without thinking, when I got to my car I took a dropperful under my tongue. My head swam with the nauseating fumes of alcohol. Looking at the label it said, 20% alcohol!

I immediately did the Mirror Technique [a technique of affirmation taught by Stu Wheelwright] saying: "I am a woman who is free from the debilitating effects of alcohol." And instantly the nausea, shock, fear and inner hunger for alcohol vanished. So did the headache.

I see the incident as a rite of passage, a proving that I am in charge of my destiny...and even though I may have...a hereditary tendency toward alcoholism (my father was an alcoholic), it's not stronger than the spiritual principles I practice.

Tears are flowing now as I realize that as Soul I am free, and at this moment, even after a year of super nutrition and therapy, I am truly free.

I'd like to express my gratitude to the important—even critical—step along the path that your nutritional program was and is even now. Looking back, I now see how you provided the supports for my own self-discovery—a gift borne of your heart, much greater than all the supplements that helped balance my biochemistry. How can I begin to say thank you?"

When people say, "All things are possible," and "Where there's a will there's a way," it is clear that human beings are unique, because we have the ability to impress the subconscious with new bioenergetic patterns that can lead to the desired life.

You may be familiar with the analogy of the tethered elephant which is particularly relevant here. Elephant trainers chain baby elephants, so the story goes, by the ankle to a strong spike in the ground. This tethers them so that they cannot wander off. At first, the baby elephant struggles against the chain, pulling on it, trying to break it. But the chain holds fast. The baby elephant learns that he cannot roam when his ankle is tethered. That information is indelibly imprinted on his famous memory.

Trainers will then be able to tether the elephant with a weak chain or rope and a small spike in the sand—something the elephant could easily break—and it will effectively keep the elephant in place.

At the circus the children often ask: "How can that little rope hold that huge elephant?" They do not know that it is not the rope, but rather belief or conditioning, that keeps the elephant tied down.

When people believe—or an even better word is KNOW—that they can live a better life without addictive activities, then they can be 100% successful in overcoming those limitations by following the principles outlined here.

1. Take the desire to be free of the addiction and cultivate it into absolute knowing that you can succeed.
2. Build a new self-image through proper use of the creative imagination. Once again, RELAX, and VISUALIZE with all your senses, and ACT AS IF you are already free.
3. Support your bioenergy with a comprehensive nutritional program of diet; nutritional supplements, such as vitamins, minerals, herbs, enzymes, amino acids; and homeopathy. A comprehensive nutritional program can help you to survive withdrawal, detoxification, and what is often misnamed "heredity," which is actually a biochemical or metabolic imbalance.
4. Support the process to become free with counseling, the Mirror Technique, and support groups, as you require, to help fine-tune your self-image and deal with self-limiting attitudes of anger or rejection, so that you can begin, once again, to grow emotionally and spiritually.

This Systemic Concept approach supports a person holistically from the top down and the bottom up, and thus provides the matrix for success. This is a matrix which the individual fills with desire and constructive efforts.

Some people doubt the power of visualization, saying that it is too esoteric. But scientists are seriously investigating this concept, and medical doctors are implementing it. The beneficial effects of visualization are well documented. A new field of research, called psychoneuroimmunology, is charting the pathways between the mind and the body, particularly in regard to stress on the immune system.

Since we have discussed the endocrine glands and the immune system in this book, here is an example how our perception of things with our minds and our experience of them with our emotions has a bearing on our energy, endocrine, and immune system.

Let's say a person goes to work on Monday, and the boss rushes in with a hot project and also needs several other things done. The person perceives this Monday morning situation as stressful, as just too much to handle.

The brain cries out: "Yikes, hypothalamus, send out the stress signal!" This activates the sympathetic branch of the autonomic nervous system which responds as told. In turn, this response causes blood to rush away from the skin, extremities, and stomach, and move to the deep muscle tissue so that self-preserving muscle responses are at maximum capacity. The body is poised to respond.

Nerve endings in the stomach and intestines release neurotransmitters/hormones. The adrenal glands release the hormone adrenaline. The high hormone level of neurotransmitters signal the adrenals to send out the hormone cortisol, which elevates sugar levels so that the body has a ready fuel supply. Cortisol also inhibits lymphocyte action to tone down the immune response.

The presence of these hormones also depresses the immune system. The Killer T-cells which fight tumors and abnormal conditions are suppressed. The net effect of reaction to stress is a weaker immune system. Reducing the immune response is a natural function. The body needs to turn off the immune system after it has done its job. An overactive immune system can result in auto-immune diseases. This is a check and balance system, but stress depletes the system.

Stress is also associated with low norepinephrine in the brain, which contributes to depression and lowers the immune response. Stress causes the thymus gland to involute (atrophy), and this reduces immune function. Stress also depletes the water soluble vitamins B-complex and C, which decreases the body's resistance to toxins and pathogens.

Further, the stress response to the type of Monday morning situation uses a great deal of energy and inhibits proper rest. So what is readily available to help the stressed person to relax, feel better, and re-engage the energy system come 8:00 a.m. Tuesday? Alcohol, tobacco, coffee, sugar, drugs! And in this way many people become addicts because of their perception of life as stressful. Just like the elephant, their freedom is limited as they become chained to an artificial, stimulating, make-it-feel-better, addictive activity. And the withdrawal symptoms reinforce the belief that such addictive action is necessary.

It is of interest that the hypothalamus initiated the stress response because it also initiates the relaxation response. And the relaxation response can be controlled by thought. People who learn to do "Mind Controlled Relaxation," "Meditation," "Contemplation," "Visualization," or what we call "Sensualization" in the publication, *Passion Play* (Tips, 1990), learn how to initiate the relaxation response instead of the stress response.

When the body is relaxed, the immune system is strong, the mind is creative, depression is overcome, and actions are effective and economical. When the body is relaxed, visualization can profoundly affect a person's life.

Healthwise, the brain, the immune system, and the endocrine system are in constant contact, initiating action, responding, and ending each others' activities in a complex system of enhancements and suppressions. The intricacies of this system are still beyond complete scientific understanding. This provides an exciting area of research that some day may eliminate drugs from the pharmacopoeia, so that health professionals will rely more on visualization and biological remedies to affect the health-building response.

SENSUALIZATION: INTRODUCTION TO THE MIRROR TECHNIQUE

In 1985, Stu Wheelwright shared with people who consulted with him a technique for impressing the subconscious with effective instructions. He felt that this technique was a short cut to obtaining tremendous personal power and could quickly lay the foundation for personal growth and success. He called it "The Mirror Technique" or "Eye of the Psyche".

Wheelwright learned the technique as part of his training to become a medicine man with the Nez Perce Indians. He explained that he was commissioned to share this technique with people, and that it was the Indians' gift to the "white eyes" for survival of the planet.

The details of the technique are spelled out in the publication, *Passion Play* (Tips, 1990). This is the textbook for the seminars in which we teach proficiency in the mirror technique.

Basically, the technique involves holding a hand mirror near the tip of your nose so that your vision shows one eye instead of two eyes. Your two eyes come together to form a single intent. You then affirm, with all your senses, the states of being and goals you wish to manifest.

According to Wheelwright, talking out loud to the mirror is a way to bypass the censors in the mind and speak directly to the subconscious "heart" of yourself. In bypassing the mind, the unceasing chatter of "I don't know," and "I can't do that," is passed over and thus cannot sabotage the pure thought of what you know you want.

The following is an example from a letter written by a seminar attendee.

Dear Jack,
Success has come quite easy with the Mirror Technique. My goal was to change an attitude that I needed "something for nothing."

Although I am basically an honest person, I had the tendency to steal a little bit. If a cashier made change in my favor, I kept it. Occasionally I would switch price tags on items I wished to buy to get a lower price. I once found a wallet and kept the money although I sent the wallet back to the person. I would often claim more hours on my time card than I actually worked. And I would pad expense account statements.

Due to my increasing spiritual awareness that such behavior was wrong for me, I still had the feeling that I needed to get an edge on life and stack the cards in my favor.

It was very difficult to stop my little attempts to balance the scales in my favor.

Recently, while shopping, I was looking at merchandise which was opened [the boxes were opened]. All I had to do to get the superior product at a reduced price was to switch boxes. Rationalizing to myself that the service was poor as no clerk was available to help me, I switched boxes and started for the check out line.

Suddenly, I thought to myself, "What am I doing? I'm stealing!" But my mind ran its usual pattern and replied, "But they owe it to me. The price was marked too high. No one helped me. Save the money and use it for something else. Life isn't fair and takes from me, now's my chance to even the score a bit."

Then, like a fresh breeze on a muggy day, my Mirror Technique affirmation came through: "I, Tom, am an honest man. I trust life to balance the scales. I am honest in all my dealings. This is what I am—100% honest!"

The merchandise virtually jumped out of my hand, back on the shelf, and I put it in the appropriate box. I left without making any purchase. I didn't really need the item, I just wanted to take advantage of my self-arranged bargain.

And from that moment on, I can guarantee you, I am 100% honest and nothing will shake that because it's who

I am! I am an honest person—no matter what, even on income tax!

Life will undoubtedly challenge my honesty again and again, but I know my values and that's how I'll live.

And it feels wonderful. I know who I am. I am definitely a freer person, just like you said. Now I trust God to balance the scales if someone steals from me. I no longer have to worry about it! That's the freedom! My mind is no longer occupied with how unfair life is and how I must seize or make opportunities to balance the scales.

I'm now starting on another Mirror Technique endeavor, this one even more profound. Someday I'll be what I already am!

The term "visualization" is not really appropriate to describe the mirror technique because it is much more than "seeing." It involves feeling, smelling, hearing, touching, tasting as well, therefore it is called "sensualization!"

For example, speaking to the single eye, I could say out loud: "I, Jack, am a man free of self-limiting and addictive activities." That is the basic, foundational statement. I could then go on to enhance that state-of-being by saying: "I feel terrific in this freedom. I have great energy and enthusiasm for living. The world sparkles to my vision, and I see clearly how to live for the good of the whole. Every taste and smell is alive and vital to my senses. Every sound rings with the essence of life. I handle my freedom with acute responsibility, ever aware that I have an impact on my family, friends, clients, and community." And so on.

Every aspect of life can be addressed via the creative mirror technique. In the publication and workshops, people define the different arenas of life they desire to improve, such as: spiritual goals; mental goals, emotional and relationship goals including parenting of children, spouse, parents; need for friends and love; and so forth. Physical goals are also addressed, such as material goods, personal wealth, and personality traits.

193

Just seven minutes a day with the mirror technique can start to mold the future and express what we want the future to hold. We are each living a perfect reflection of what we expect and what our attitudes dictate. If we have limitations in our lives, it is because that is what we expect subconsciously. It is what we have created for ourselves. With the mirror technique we can start to implement constructive change in our lives. By working with the mirror technique we can break addictions and replace them with positive attitudes and activities. We can grow, learn, and enjoy everything in life!

To further enhance the power of the mirror technique, a person can visualize or "sensualize" a specific point from the mirror technique exercise. Here is a specific exercise I learned from a remarkable lady, who is a counselor for prison inmates in Austin. Here's how it goes. Set aside a private, undisturbed time. Relax. Be still. Close your eyes. Start to experience with your mind's eye.

See yourself walking into an old fashioned school room. Hear your feet echo on the hard wood floor. Smell the familiar odors of books. Look around at the individual, flip-top desks and the sturdy oak teacher's desk in front of the room. The desk has a piece of fruit on it. Behind the teacher's desk is a large, clean chalk board and a new piece of chalk. Pick up the chalk. Feel its smooth surface and fine powder on your fingers.

Now write on the chalk board a list of all the addictions you'd like to let drop away. Anything that limits your freedom and happiness. Include self-limiting emotional states such as guilt and fear. While you are writing, a man approaches you. Love and compassion radiate from him. Your eyes meet his and there is instant recognition on his kind face. A soft blue light fills the room. The air rings with peace as you hug this being. His head nods with approval as you turn back to the chalk board to review and finish your list.

As you finish your list, the man picks up an eraser of brilliant blue light and begins to erase your list. You feel lighter and lighter as each letter and word completely disappears.

Now, the board is completely erased. The man takes the piece of fruit off the teacher's desk and you eat it, tasting the delightful, vital freshness. You feel its wonderful nutrients replacing the void the addictions once filled.

In gratitude, you leave the room and return to your new life.

YOU CAN DO IT!

I know you can quit your addictions, because I have seen so many others overcome their addictions by using the techniques outlined in this book. There is, however, no substitute for your sincere desire to change the way in which you get your energy. But rather than beating yourself over the head about being an addict or casually involved with addictive activities, just acknowledge that your addiction springs from a lack of genuine energy. Now, after reading this book, you know how to get the real energy.

Many great things are in store for you as you take each step towards self-mastery.

I have enjoyed visiting with you and providing you the details of natural therapies to overcome addictions as well as any other limitation in life. Now the action is up to you!

BIBLIOGRAPHY

Achterberg, Jean. *Imagery in Healing*. Boston: Shambhala, 1985.

Atkins, Robert C. *Dr. Atkin's Health Revolution*. Boston: Houghton Miffling, 1989.

Bach, Edward. *The Bach Flower Remedies,* 1952. Reprint. New Canaan, CT: Keats Publishing, Inc., 1977.

Becker, Robert O. *Cross Currents. The Promise of Electromedicine, the Perils of Electropollution.* Los Angeles: Jeremy P. Tarcher Inc., 1990.

Cheraskin, E. & W. M. Ringsdorf. *Psychodietetics.* Toronto: Bantam Books, 1974.

Gerber, Richard. *Vibrational Medicine.* Santa Fe, NM: Bear & Co., 1988.

Lesser, Michael. *Nutrition and Vitamin Therapy.* Toronto: Bantam Books, 1981.

Milam & Ketcham. *Under The Influence. A Guide to the Myth and Realities of Alcoholics.* Seattle: Madrona Publishers, 1981.

Morter, M. T. "Implications of pH in Urinalysis." In Yanick, Paul, Jr. & Russell Jaffe, eds. *Clinical Chemistry & Nutrition Guidebook.* T&H Publishing, 1988.

Ott, John. *Light, Radiation & You.* Greenwich, CT: Devin-Adair, Publishers, 1985.

Phelps, Janice Keller & Alan E. Nourse. *The Hidden Addiction and How to Get Free.* Boston: Little, Brown and Company, 1986.

Robinson, Bryan E. *Work Addiction: Hidden Legacies of Adult Children.* Deerfield Beach, FL: Health Communications Inc., 1989.

Selye, Hans. *The Stress of Life.* Rev. Ed. New York: McGraw-Hill, 1976.

Sheldrake, Rupert. *A New Science of Life: The Hypothesis of Formative Causation.* London: Blond & Briggs, 1981.

_____. *The Presence of the Past. Morphic Resonance and the Habits of Nature,* New York: Vintage Books, 1988.

Siegel, Bernie S. *Peace, Love & Healing.* N.Y.: Harper & Row, 1989.

Tips, Jack. *Conquer Candida and Restore Your Immune System.* 2nd ed. Austin, TX: Insight Press, 1989.

_____. *The Liver Triad.* 2nd ed. Austin, TX: Insight Press, 1989.

_____. *ProVita! Diet.* 3rd ed. Austin, TX: Insight Press, 1989.

Twitchell, Paul. *Herbs the Magic Healers.* 2nd ed. Chrystal, MN: Illuminated Way Publishing, 1988.

Wheelwright, A. Stuart. "Quantum Chemistry—Healing Beyond Herbology." Lecture. Ogden, Utah, 1985.

ABOUT THE AUTHOR _____

Jacks Tips, ND, PhD CCN, CHom., brings the message of health through nutrition to thousands through lectures, workshops, articles, radio, books and television. His background beginning in 1971 includes studies with many of the world's renowned health leaders — Dr. Bernard Jensen (iridology, naturopathy), Dr. Wilhelm Langreder (German nosode homeopathy), A.S. Wheelwright, (systemic herbology, bioenergetic nutrition, sclerology), Stanley Burroughs (cleansing diet, color therapy), Dr. Paul Eck (biochemical mineral ratios), Dr. Alan Beardall (kinesiology), Dr. Robin Murphy (classical homeopathy) and many others including the Occidental Institute Research Foundation (electro-acupuncture) in Vancouver, B.C. In 1980, Mr. Tips began consulting in the applications of systemic herbology, homeopathy, and clinical nutrition. He holds a doctorate in Naturopathy (N.D. — a 2-year program) as well as a Ph.D. in Nutrition Science from the Roger Williams School of Nutrition Science — Clayton University (Clayton, Missouri). His dissertation, "Conquer Candida" has received international recognition as a definitive work on natural cure and the challenges of the immune system. He has attained the CHom credential from the Hahnemann Academy of North America for training in classical homeopathy. He holds certification as a nutritional counselor (CCN) and serves on the board of directors of the Texas Chapter of the International and American Association of Clinical Nutritionists. He is a Fellow of the American Council of Applied Clinical Nutritionists (FACACN). Currently he is the president of the International Sclerology Foundation, and with his wife, Janine, operates the Apple-A-Day Clinic in Austin, Texas. Here he consults with people both in person and by phone, and conducts a training program for health professionals by phone on the applications of Dr. Wheelwright's formulas.

Inquiries and comments to the author are encouraged and may be made in care of the publisher:

Apple-A-Day Press
4201 Bee Caves Road, Suite C212
Austin, Texas 78746-6458
(512) 328-3996

APPLE-A-DAY PRESS

BOOKS

THE PRO-VITA! PLAN FOR OPTIMAL NUTRITION
by *Jack Tips*

At last! A way to build health based on both biochemistry and bioenergy! An extraordinary overview of how to minimize stress and maximize assimilation of essential nutrients: vegetables, low-stress protein, essential oils, and carbohydrates. A safe, non-radical nutritional foundation for your healing program, abundant health, greater energy and longevity. Daily nutrition plans and delicious recipes are included. Learn how to design the optimal nutrition meal. You will gain a greater understanding of nutrition and its role in health. A simple approach to more energy, weight loss, improved immunity, and better health! 376 pages, index, ISBN 0-929167-05-8 (**$19.95**)

CONQUER CANDIDA—RESTORE YOUR IMMUNE SYSTEM
by *Jack Tips*

An in-depth look at this health-undermining pandemic that contributes to allergies, chronic fatigue, PMS, chronic infections, headaches, bloating, memory loss, and immune deficiency. Explains what to do about these conditions by indicating causes and offering unique insights based on hundreds of clinical case histories. This information goes beyond current treatments and offers an understanding of how to conquer candida. 163 pages, ISBN 0-929167-00-7 (**$13.95**)

THE NEXT STEP TO GREATER ENERGY — A Unique Perspective on Bioenergy, Addictions and Transformation.
by *Jack Tips*

Explore the energy systems of the body with emphasis on the glandular (thyroid and adrenals) and bioelectric energy systems. This book presents a new look at the connection between bioenergy and addictions. Discover energy impostors including substances, activities, and habits. Identify addictions and habits as symptoms of bioenergetic and biochemical imbalances. Discover the true cause of cravings and addictive patterns, and how to correct the underlying imbalances. How to stop smoking is thoroughly discussed. The focus of this practical information is how to obtain freedom and fuller spiritual expression. When you are ready for change, you are ready for THE NEXT STEP! 210 pages, index, ISBN 0-929167-04-X (**$14.95**)

YOUR LIVER—YOUR LIFELINE! by Jack Tips

A fascinating look at the liver—your most important organ—its bioforces and the Chinese healing system involving the triad of the liver-stomach-colon. Explains in easy steps how to detoxify your liver and entire body the natural way. Contains provocative insights into how herbs work, natural liver treatments and cures. 150 pages, illustrations, photos, index, ISBN 0-929167-06-6 (**$11.95**)

COOKING WITH BROOKE Recipes by Melane Lohmann

Delicious Pro-Vita! recipes served by Brooke Medicine Eagle at the Eagle Song Camp (Blacktail Ranch, Montana) 57 pages, spiral bound, illustrated (**$10.00**)

WOMEN'S HEALTH DISCOURSES by Jack Tips

1) **PMS** — Features a questionnaire for physical and emotional symptoms, and a guide to using emotional symptoms to design a complete nutritional program. Discusses the subject with insights few professionals consider.

2) **A Systemic Approach to Menopause** — The myths of menopause and how nutrition can help avoid the need for estrogen replacement. Provides programs for hot flashes, flooding, calcium utilization, insomnia and other post-menopausal conditions.

3) **Osteoporosis: The Preventable Disease** — A discussion of the causes and prevention of this disease, the osteoporosis equation, and an osteoporosis risk survey.

4) **Breast Health** — The breast massage technique and its role in overall female endocrine health and the prevention of disease.

60 pages, all four discourses (**$19.95**)

BREAST HEALTH (Women's Health Discourses #4) by Jack Tips

A reprint of the Breast Health chapter of Women's Health Discourses on the role of breast tissue in female endocrine balance. Features the breast massage technique to help prevent breast disease. 26 pages, (**$7.95**)

FOR THE HEALTH PROFESSIONAL

*These materials are designed for the practicing health professional,
but are available to everyone.*

BLOOD CHEMISTRY & CLINICAL NUTRITION
by Jack Tips

For the clinical nutritionist, this manual examines each blood test value
from the SMAC-26/CBC lab test for its nutritional health implications
and provides protocols for correcting imbalances. Includes optimal values,
pathologies, clinical notes, and insights from other clinicians. An absolutely
essential tool for the practicing health professional. 123 pages, cross-
references, notebook, ISBN 0-929167-07-4 (**$44.95**)

A GUIDEBOOK TO CLINICAL NUTRITION FOR THE HEALTH PROFESSIONAL *by Timothy Kuss*

A fascinating guide through Dr. Wheelwright's work with herbs. Includes
a 400-entry Clinician's Manual and demonstrates Dr. Wheelwright's
bioenergetic research. Full of valuable information on the natural cure of
the most common health concerns. 241 pages (**$18.95**)

SYSTEMIC NUTRITION TRAINING PROGRAM
by Jack Tips with Tim Kuss

For the health professional, this training program features 14 cassette
tapes, and a 200-page manual for comprehensive training in the applications
of Dr. Wheelwright's Research and Systemic Herbal Formulas. (**$159.00**)

THE SYSTEMIC CONCEPT: Introduction to Systemic Formulas
by Jack Tips

A discussion on the genius of Dr. Stuart Wheelwright and how he
formulated bioenergetic, self-limiting herbal products based on the natural
laws of health and healing. (**$9.95**)

SCLEROLOGY

The art and science of interpreting the red lines in the white of the eye.

INSIGHTS IN THE EYES: An Introduction To Sclerology *by Jack Tips*

A thorough introduction to the history, premises, and practice of interpreting the red lines in the white of the eyes for stress patterns and nutritional implications. Features the 30 most common stress lines. 70 pages. (**$19.95**)

THE ART & SCIENCE OF SCLEROLOGY CERTIFICATION COURSE *by Jack Tips*

This course will certify you to interpret what the sclera—the white of the eyes—is saying about a person's health. It contains seven hours of instructional video tapes along with a segment on adrenal glands taught by Dr. Stuart Wheelwright; a wall chart suitable for framing; an acetate overlay system to assist practitioners in charting; and the certification examination. Upon successful completion of the exam, your certificate will be issued by the International Sclerology Foundation. (**$399**)

SCLEROLOGY VIDEO

Presents an overview of Sclerology and a demonstration of how to chart the eyes. (**$24.95**)

SCLEROLOGY WALL CHART

Sclerology is the art of evaluating health stresses from the red lines in the white of the eyes. Chart outlines zones and lines. Artfully designed, 9"x12", laminated. (**$8.95**)

Apple-A-Day Press
(512) 328-3996
FAX (512) 328-0812
4201 Bee Caves Road, Suite C-212
Austin, Texas 78746-6458

(Include $3.95 shipping for one item plus $1.00 for each additional item.)
MasterCard, VISA, Checks, C.O.D.

NOTICE TO HEALTH PROFESSIONALS

Apple-A-Day Natural Health Services offers a training program in Systemic Herbology and the Natural Laws of Life. The program consists of a 14-hour cassette training program with a 200-page manual, phone conference training with Dr. Tips, and a phone or fax hot line for program design for your patients and clients.

Please contact Apple-A-Day at (512) 328-3996 for more information.

Index

Arsenic, 157
Arteriosclerosis, 96
Arthritis, 89, 174
Artificial stimulation, 66, 67-68, 146
Aspartame, 75
Asthma, 64, 86
Atkins, Robert, 87
Auric field, 98-99

Bach, Edward, 40-41, 152
Bach Flower Remedies, 40-41, 152, 162
Barley Green, 175
Becker, Robert O., 2, 10
Beethoven, Ludwig van, 128
Bergson, Henry, 2
Beta waves, 127
Biochemistry
    of adrenal glands, 63-65
    of alcohol, 107, 113-120
    of caffeine addiction, 77-79
    of chocolate addiction, 86-87
    of cocaine, 133-136
    of immune response, 66-67
    of stress response, 53-54
    in study of addictions, 5
    of sugar addiction, 72-73
    synergistic relationship with bioenergy in the
        whole person, 5-10, 43
    of thyroid gland, 62-63
Bioenergetic sciences. See also Acupuncture;
    Homeopathy
    compared with Western views of body, 4, 5, 9
    examples of, 5
    medical insurance and, 8-9, 16
    opposition to, 7, 8, 9, 25
Bioenergy
    common items disruptive of, 10-13
    definition of, 2
    examples of the bioenergetic effect, 10-13
    health triad and, 31-32
    and holistic model of health, 21-23
    marijuana and, 98-99
    philosophical history from Eastern and
        Western
    traditions, 2-4
    positive and negative flow of, 2, 3-4
    relationship with addictions, 1-2, 13-17
    sciences for the study of, 5, 6
    synergistic relationship with biochemistry in
        the whole person, 5-10, 43
    types of energy, 38
Biokinesiology, 55-56
Bioscientific sciences, opposition to, 104
Birth defects, 111
Blood sugar levels, 64, 66, 72, 156. See also
    Hypoglycemia

Blood tests
    SMAC-25 blood test, 56-57
    for thyroid function, 70
Blu green algae, 175
Blum, Kenneth, 119, 131
Boron, 80
Brain
    alcohol use and, 114-120
    alpha and beta waves in, 127
    cocaine use and, 133-136
Bush, Kate, 127

Cactus Grand, 152
Cadmium, 68, 93, 144, 146, 157
Caffeinated sodas, 81-82
Caffeine
    adrenals and, 65
    artificial stimulation and, 68
    biochemistry of, 77-79
    caffeinated sodas, 81-82
    in coffee, 77-81
    danger level of, 83
    effects of, 27, 78-79
    effects of stopping the use of, 83-85
    interference with action of natural therapies,
        80-81
    level of harm of, 40
    nutritional deficiencies and, 172
    as pseudo energy addiction, 34, 39, 54
    in tea, 81
    withdrawal symptoms, 20, 78, 79
Calcitonin, 62
Calcium, 139
Canabis Sativa 200C, 100
Cancer, 77, 92-95, 99, 107, 108, 154-155, 174
Candida albicans infections, 66, 74, 174
Carbohydrates, 163
Cardiovascular disease, 123
Catecholamines, 79
Cellulase, 153
Cerebellum, degeneration of, 110
Change, desire for, 43
Cheek, cancer of, 94
Chemicals, 104-106
Cheraskin, D., 156
Ch'i, 2, 126
Child abuse, 112
Chinese tradition, 2, 7
Chiropractic, 8-9
Chlordane, 104
Chlorella, 175
Chocolate
    as allergenic substance, 85-86
    artificial stimulation and, 68
    caffeine contained in, 79
    clinical case histories concerning, 29-30

Ga herbal formula, 69, 169
GABA, 118, 168
Gardens Alive, 105
Gastric ulcers, 109
Gastritis, 109
Gb herbal formula, 162
Gerber, Richard, 2, 8, 14
Germany, 7, 8
Gf herbal formula, 70, 162
Glucocorticoids, 64
Gluconeogenesis, 63
GOLD herbal formula, 41, 101, 162
Goldenseal, 101
Great Britain, 7
Green Magma, 175
Greenlife, 175
Grief, 35

Hahnemann, Samuel, 8, 24
Hair test, 55, 69, 74, 149
Harris, Jon, 125
Health
    definition of, 3, 6, 21
    health triad, 16, 31-32, 67
    holistic model of, 21-23
Health food industry, 73, 76
Health triad, 16, 31-32, 67
Heart attacks, 95
Heart disease, 79
Hepatitis, 110, 113
Herbicides, 104
Herbology, 5, 7, 25. See also Systemic herbology
Heroin, 33, 34, 40, 51, 65, 107, 116, 135
Holistic, definition of, 9
Holistic model of health, 21-23
Homeopathic remedies
    holistic health model and, 21-22
    opposition to, 104
    plants' energy and, 8
    for stop smoking programs, 151-152, 161-
        162
    success of, 7-8
Homeopathy
    definition of, 5, 7
    effectiveness of, 7-8, 174-175
    founding of, 8
    opposition to, 8, 25
    and treatment of addictions, 23-26
Human beings
    bioenergetic pattern for, 15
    and holistic model of health, 18-23
    model of, 3-4
    positive and negative flow of energy in, 2, 3-4
    synergistic relationship between bioenergy
        and biochemistry in, 5-10, 43

Humulus, 162
Hyperthyroidism, 63
Hypnotism, 169
Hypoglycemia, 55, 64, 72, 73, 86, 93, 156, 163
Hypothalamus, 53, 66, 72, 163, 189, 190
Hypothyroidism, 62-63, 70

"I need" syndrome, 44-45
Ignatia, 162
Ignatia Amara, 152
Imaging, 183-191
Immune system
    addictions and, 65-68
    adrenal glands and, 64-65
    causal chain and, 61
    marijuana use and, 99-100
    pesticides and, 106
    stress and, 54, 189-190
    sugar craving and, 74
    tobacco and, 145
    visualization and, 189
Impotency, 111
Inorganic salt, 88-89, 90
Inositol, 168
Insecticide Detox, 104
Insecticides, 104-106
Insulin, 72
Insurance. See Medical insurance
Integrative Breathing, 180-181
International Sclerology Foundation, 71
Interro testing device, 104
Invertase, 153
Iron, 81

Japanese tradition, 38
Jogging, excessive, 124-125

Kali Bichromium, 29
Kali Phos, 152
Keener-Clark, Jessie, 179-182
Ketchum, 108
Ki, 2
Killer T-cells, 189
Kinesiology, applied, 55-56
Koop, Everett, 103
Kreb's cycle, 121, 170

L-glutamine, 119, 168
L-phenylalanine, 168
L-tryptophan, 119, 168
L-tyrosine, 119
Larynx, cancer of, 94
Laughing gas, 35, 37-38
Leahy, Senator, 106
Lecithin, 151, 168
Lesser, Michael, 152

Leukoplakia, 93
Life force, 2-4, 38
Lighting, 10-13
Lip, cancer of, 94
Lipase, 153
Lithium, 173
Liver, 72, 107, 113, 145
Liver, fatty, 110
Liver Triad Program, 11, 29, 67, 107, 113, 145, 162
Lobelia Avenasativa, 152
Loeblich, Laurel A., 131
Loud rock 'n' roll music, 127-130, 145-146
Lung cancer, 92-93, 154-155

Ma-huang, 164
Magnesium, 85, 139
Magnetic energy, 38
Malathion, 104, 105, 106
Maltase, 153
Marijuana
    adrenals and, 65
    artificial stimulation and, 68
    case histories concerning, 27-28, 100-101
    cocaine addiction and, 135
    effects of, 27, 37, 93, 97-100
    long-term residues remaining in body, 96-97, 101
    as medicinal herb, 101
    metaphysical aspects of, 97-98
    nutritional deficiencies and, 172
    personal experiences with, 45-46
    proponents of, 102
    stress and, 52
Massage, 52, 123
Medical insurance, 8-9, 16
Meridian energy, 38
Methamphetamine, 34, 51
Methylene chloride, 77, 78
Microwave ovens, 13
Milam, 108
Mineral supplements, 74, 159-161
Mirror Technique, 187, 188, 191-195
Mononucleosis, 113
Mormon Tea, 164
Morphine, 34, 36, 116
Morter, M. T., 142
Moschus, 162
Mozart, Amadeus, 128
Murder, 112
Music, rock 'n' roll, 127-130, 145-146

Naloxone, 78
Narcotics Anonymous, 138
Nausea, 101
Nc herbal formula, 169

"Need syndrome, 44-45
Negative energy, in human body, 2, 3-4
Neuralgia, 89
Neuritis, 89, 110
Newtonian physics, 14
Niacin, 168
Nicotine. See Tobacco
Nitrous oxide, 35, 37-38
Norepinephrine, 78, 118, 190
Norpremin, 173
Nourse, A. E., 73, 96
Nutrasweet, 75-77
Nutrition. See also Pro-Vita! Diet
    acidity/alkalinity, 152-153, 175
    addictions and nutritional deficiencies, 171-176
    addictions as symptoms of imbalance, 57-60
    alcohol and, 114-120
    beneficial and detrimental dietary energy, 41-43
    cellular energy and, 38
    excessive weight and, 87
    light perspective on, 170-171
    recovery from cocaine addiction, 139-140
    role in energy addictions, 144
    salt, 88-91
    for smokers, 156-161
    Standard American Diet (SAD), 175
    for stop smoking program, 150-154, 161-163, 167-169
    support for breaking addictions, 176-177
Nutritional supplements, 159-161
Nux Vomica, 100, 152, 162

Obesity, 86
Opium, 34
Organic farming, 106
Organic salt, 88, 89, 91
Orgasm, 125-127
Orr, Leonard, 180
Orthene, 106
Orthomolecular psychiatrists, 152
Orthostatic hypotension, 69
Osteoporosis, 82, 174
Ott, John, 11
Overwork. See Working, compulsive
Oxalic acid, 77
Oxidase, 153

Pachebel, 128
Pain relief addictions, 34-36, 41. See also Alcohol; Cocaine; Heroin; Morphine; Tobacco
Pancreas, 72
Pancreatitis, 109
Parathormone, 62
Passiflora, 162

Peroxidase, 153
Pesticides, 104-106
Pfaffia, 80
pH, 65
pH tests, 175
Pharynx, cancer of, 94
Phelps, J. K., 73, 96
Phenylethylamine, 59
Phosphatase, 153
Phosphoric acid, 82
Pituitary gland, 53, 66, 72, 163
Polonium, 157
Positive energy, in human body, 2, 3-4
Pregnancy, and marijuana use, 100
Prescription drugs, 173-174
Pro-Vita! Diet, 11, 29, 42-43, 53, 59, 73, 90, 123, 124-125, 163, 168, 170
Protease, 153
Pseudo energy addictions, 34, 36-39, 41-43, 65 67. See also Alcohol; Caffeine; Chocolate; Compulsive activities; Sugar; Tobacco
Psychoneuroimmunology, 189
Pyridoxal-5-phosphate, 168
Pyrogenium, 29

Quiz on addictions, 48-52

Radiation, 10, 11, 14
Radionics testing device, 104
Rastafarians, 98-99
Reacreational drugs. See Marijuana; Cocaine; and names of other drugs
Reflexology, 8, 126
Rescue, 162
Rheumatism, 89
Ritalin, 173
Roberts, H. R., 75
Robinson, Bryan, 121-122
Rock 'n' roll music, 127-130, 145-146
Rotation diets, 87
Round-up, 104, 105

Salt, excessive, 68, 88-91
Salt free diets, 89
Salt water baths, 90
Sanpaku, 38
Sclerology, 70-71, 126
Sea salt, 90
Selenium, 157
Self-love, 180-182
Selye, Hans, 52-53
Sensualization, 190, 191-195
Sepia 9c, 11
Serotonin, 118, 163
Sheldrake, Rupert, 3
Shiatsu, 8

Siegel, Bernie, 184
Silicea, 25, 29, 100
Single working parents, 123
SMAC-25 blood test, 56-57
Smith, J. J., 114
Smoke, and nonsmokers, 155-156
Smoking. See Stop smoking program; Tobacco
Sodas, caffeinated, 81-82
Sodium, 88, 89
Soul, 4
Speed, 34, 40
Spiritual dimension, 4, 20-21, 36, 45
Sputum cytology, 154
Standard American Diet (SAD), 175
Steroids, 33, 63-64
Stomach ulcers, 96
Stop smoking program. See also Tobacco
    design of a plan for, 165-169
    hypnotism and, 169
    listing reasons for stopping, 165-166
    new behavior patterning, 147-149
    nutrition for, 161-163, 167-169
    ruling out cancer, 154-155
    setting date for stopping, 166-167
    smoke and nonsmokers, 155-156
    stress management, 149-154
    stress of stopping smoking, 164-165
    weight gain and, 163-164
Stravinski, Igor, 128
Stress
    alcoholism and, 116, 117
    biochemistry of, 52-55
    causal chain and, 61
    immune system and, 189-190
    nutrition and, 175
    of stopping smoking, 164-165
Stress management, in stop smoking program, 149-154
Sugar
    biochemistry of sugar addiction, 72-73
    in cafeinated sodas, 82
    in children of alcoholics, 107
    clinical case histories concerning, 27-30
    effects of, 27, 40, 55, 68, 72
    mineral supplementation and, 74
    natural sugar substitutes, 73, 76-77
    Nutrasweet as substitute for, 75-77
    nutritional deficiencies and, 172
    per capita consumption of, 74
    as pseudo energy addiction, 34, 39, 54
    stigma attached to, 48-49
    test for debilitating effects of, 55-56
    thyroid's role in sugar use by body, 63
Suicide, 112
Sulphur, 100
Suma, 80

For more information about the programs discussed in this book, contact your Natural Health Professional: